Guidelines 4

Implementing Individualised Learning

in schools and colleges

W J K Davies

Council for Educational Technology

Published by the Council for Educational Technology,
3 Devonshire Street, London W1N 2BA

First published 1978
ISBN 0 902204-73-4
ISSN 0308-0323

 British Library Cataloguing in Publication Data

Davies, William James Keith
Implementing Individualised Learning. –
(Council for Educational Technology for the United
Kingdom. Guidelines 4; 0309-0323).
1. Individualised instruction. 2. Education,
Secondary – 1965– 3. Individualised instruction.
I. Title. II. Series.
373.1'3'94   LB1031
ISBN 0-902204-73-4

Printed in Great Britain by
H Cave & Company Limited
Cumberland Street,
Leicester LE1 4QQ

Contents

Preface

This book is intended for teachers and departmental teaching teams who are finding themselves in a position where they need to consider problems of providing differential work for students within single class-sized groups — typically in a mixed-ability situation; it is biased to secondary/further education. The premise is that the reader has some pressure on him or some interest in moving from a formal teaching situation towards individualised work patterns.

The book is intended as a practical introduction to the problems of initiating various forms of individualised or resource-oriented work. It does not set out to be self-sufficient but intends to pose the major problems, to give the teacher practice in considering solutions, and to put forward some aids to dealing with the situations that may arise.

Since it must be considered as a reference guide, the major part is in plain prose — though structured for easy retrieval; since, however, any individualised learning approach involves concepts of material design with which the teacher may not be familiar, extensions of the main argument are presented by pieces of structured individual work material of various kinds. These are designed as optional extras and the integrity of the book as a piece of advice does not *depend* on the reader using them.

Author's acknowledgements

If this book has a parentage, it is a union of the work carried out over the past ten years or so in the writer's unit with the ideas and suggestions acquired over the same period by meeting other people in the same line of work.

I am extremely grateful to my own colleagues and all those with whom my work has brought me into contact — in education, in industry, in the armed services. Three in particular, Mr J H Embling OBE, Mr M Edmundson HMI and my colleague Mrs M Needham have been particularly helpful and critical in savaging the manuscript until it assumed a reasonable shape. The ideas and thoughts contained therein have come from sources too numerous to list. Last, but by no means least, Dawn Law typed the manuscript . . . and modified the typed manuscript to take account of all the changes.

W J K Davies,
Director,
County Programmed Learning Centre,
St Albans, Hertfordshire.

1. What's in a Phrase?

What indeed? Educational jargon abounds in beautiful-sounding phrases, however, and the area this book considers is fuller of them than most. 'Resource-based learning', 'independent learning systems', 'student-oriented activities', 'individualised learning experiences'. There is a positive plethora all with only one thing in common — the idea that any phrase that includes the words 'class', 'group', 'teaching', must necessarily be dull, old-fashioned and out of date. Otherwise they all have new and essentially different concepts to offer; indeed anyone can form his or her own definition.

In fact you might like to start this book by picking out the definition that most nearly fits your idea of what we are talking about. To help you here is an instant word list of the 15 most popular words.

STUDENT	ORIENTED	LEARNING
TEACHER	BASED	TEACHING
LEARNER	ASSISTED	ACTIVITIES
RESOURCE	CENTRED	EXPERIENCES
INDEPENDENT		
INDIVIDUALISED		
GROUP		

Just pick the ones that make up the concept of what you think we are talking about and then string them together.

Since you picked them you presumably have a clear idea of what you mean — or do you? What is 'resource-based learning'? or 'individual learning activities'? For that matter what is 'independent' work and what is a 'resource'? So many different meanings have been attached to these words that it is difficult to use them meaningfully without misinterpretation. Perhaps, therefore, we might start by considering briefly what we are talking about. We can at least *group* the semantic labels which may cut down the confusion. Thus:

— learning
— teaching
— activities
— experiences

all simply say that something is going on, ie, an activity of some sort is taking place.

If we look at them more closely, 'activities' and 'experiences' are not very informative unless qualified — and well qualified at that. They are not specifically associated with the learning process and unfortunately are often used by people who are vague about what they are trying to say; if you used either in your definition you need to ask yourself exactly *what* you mean. *Teaching* and *learning*, on the other hand, are fairly well-established labels; exact interpretations may vary but in general *teaching* implies the deliberate passing on of skills, knowledge, opinions, etc, by one person to another, while *learning* implies acquisition of skills, etc, by a person through his own efforts. In this context, therefore, we are indicating whether what we are talking about has a strong didactic element or is mainly the responsibility of the person learning. An interesting if rather sneaky variation label that has grown up is 'teaching/learning' implying presumably that the activity concerned has elements of both and as a piece of shorthand it seems reasonable.

Since both teaching and learning also imply *doing* something there seems little advantage if you talk about 'teaching activities' etc, in this context though some might claim that a 'learning experience' is more definite.

Secondly there are:

— group
— individualised
— independent

the first two of these describe people-patterns, the way in which work can be organised to cope with differing numbers and types of students. Of the three, 'group' is the most self-explanatory — a number of people organised to work together. You only need to clarify for yourself what kind of group you mean — a class? a homogeneous cluster of three . . . four . . . eight . . . people? a 'seminar' of ten or fifteen? Is it led or does it make its own collective decisions? These problems may not seem important but they are when you have to design an educational situation in detail. 'Individualised' is clearly the opposite of 'group' in that it implies that the work has been adapted or designed for use by individuals but that is all the word does imply. It is, however, interpreted in various ways, often being taken as almost synonymous with 'learning' and implying that *all* the work is designed for single students; yet one can certainly have individual teaching and the term *has* been widened to include relevant pair and small-group activities. Perhaps the most sensible interpretation is that it simply indicates that attention has been paid to problems likely to be encountered by separate students rather than by 'students-in-a-mass'.

'Individualised' is often confused with 'independent' but they are not the same thing at all, although 'individualised learning', and 'independent' learning are often thought of as identical. 'Independent' surely describes a state of being; it indicates that the person so described can decide his own course of action, can do what he wants when he wants to. True, it is normally linked with learning rather than teaching and implies work by an individual because in any group there must be some constraint on each person's freedom of action; yet it is worth noting that in practice much of what people call 'independent' work may be guided and involve collaborative activities. The point is that while independent work is likely to be individual(ised), individualised work is by no means necessarily independent and may be quite rigidly teacher-controlled.

Lastly, we come to the more complex set of labels which indicate the ways in which teaching or learning may be approached:

— student ⎫   ⎧ oriented
— learner ⎪   ⎪ based
— teacher ⎬   ⎨ *centred*
— resource ⎭   ⎩ assisted

All in some combination describe a condition or bias within the learning process. All are lovely emotive words which trigger off different visions in different people but in essence they simply encompass a range of approaches in which the focal point (for information, expertise, action) is either a person or some other source.

The major problematic element, in semantic terms, is the word 'resource' and this is only because it has been interpreted in so many different ways of which the broadest is 'anything associated with the learning process'. In practice this latter is such a wide definition that people often use the term much more narrowly according to their sectional interests (eg, an audio-visual aids specialist says it is his machines and software; a librarian may say resources are simply non-book information materials). The danger in both extremes is that for different reasons they tend not to have much meaning. In the first case one has a tendency not to think further because by definition everything one does is resource-based; in the second case the definition is so narrow that 'resources' get regarded simply as peripheral aids to be grafted on to whatever a teacher is doing at a given time. It may be preferable to label as a resource something or someone that can be identified as useful in extending or facilitating learning in a particular situation and which is deliberately included.

In this context we can then think of a resource as being anything that actually contributes to the learning process at any given time and that therefore has definite attributes in terms of usefulness for specific purposes; ability to be modified to suit different people's needs; appropriateness. It might either be a physical object of some kind (including a person!) or it might be a means of facilitating learning activity by doing something to modify the environment or milieu in which learning is taking place — say an alteration in timetabling or a reorganisation of the room spaces in part of a school or college. So it may be a *thing* or an *activity*. Let us for the moment just call the two categories:

physical resources: objects, raw materials, tools, sources of information

organisational resources: timetabling decisions, team-teaching organisation, planning for various activities.

So at the end if we ignore the blanket words like 'activities', 'experiences', etc, we come to the idea that any educational situation (teaching and/or learning) is composed essentially of four 'dimensions' that can interact on each other. The diagram below shows them graphically — note that the word

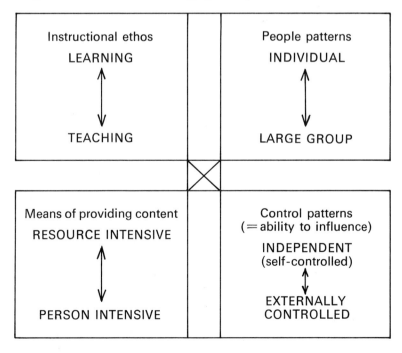

'situation' is being used strictly in its dictionary sense. These have been set out like this because it is the labels in capitals that people usually identify. Yet really each dimension is not a black/white choice but a whole range of choices. Take for instance the 'people-patterns' involved. Put even fairly crudely the range is more like —

INDIVIDUAL
PAIR
SMALL COLLABORATIVE GROUP
'SEMINAR' GROUP (say 8–15)
CLASS GROUP
LARGE GROUP

These patterns are not mutually exclusive so several can exist at the same time, but they all have their own characteristics. You might like to try roughly delineating the other ranges of options before looking at the table opposite.

Instructional ethos	Control pattern	People patterns	Means of providing content
LEARNING (free learning) guided learning	INDEPENDENT cooperative collaborative	INDIVIDUAL	RESOURCE INTENSIVE (based) resources aided by person (teacher)
mutual exploration	guided		
informal teaching	internally directed or controlled (by 'teacher')		person aided by resources
formal teaching	EXTERNALLY CONTROLLED (eg, by exam requirements)		
TEACHING		LARGE GROUP	PERSON INTENSIVE (teacher as resource)

It is true that the 'instructional ethos' column is perhaps a little simplistic. It could be more clearly expressed as a combination of teaching and learning approaches as shown below from teacher's and learner's point of view. In practice, however, we are looking at the matter only from your point of view, as the teacher, and so the less complex version is likely to provide what we need.

TEACHING APPROACH	DEGREE OF INFLUENCE	LEARNING APPROACH
didactic teaching		passive absorption
guiding		mainly helped
collaborating		collaborating
supervising		some guidance
standing by		active learning

So one might liken these dimensions to a set of dimmers on a stage lighting installation. They are not on/off switches but have variable settings and by altering one or more of the settings it is possible to change the effect on the audience — the students. This is not, of course, to say that the teacher is always the person who decides where to position the knobs! The student may do it; external factors may dictate what sort of educational situation is set up; the settings may not be a consciously thought-out choice at all; but they will determine what the audience sees.

We must note, too, that all these dimensions are interconnected. Just as in a lighting plot, altering any one alters the effect of others — and may indeed change their effectiveness as part of the whole scene. Fashions tend to concentrate on one easy semantic label, eg, *'resource-based* (work)'. It is all too easy not to think what this means in terms of the other dimensions if an effective educational process is to take place.

Yet, particularly as one gets away from the 'well-known' end of the range (group teaching with the teacher as major provider) so comparatively small changes in ethos may require corresponding — or even more marked — changes in how to provide content or what numbers of students can be handled; conversely the number of students allocated to a teacher may have great effects on how far he can organise his instructional ethos.

In practice, of course, none of these dimensions is static — or at least not for very long. Any educational situation is constantly changing both in the long term (eg, new skills) and in the short term (eg, student concentration span; different tasks needing different activities) so that you need to plan in advance and constantly adjust your settings. This is important because it shows the weakness of fashionable generalisations — the more generalised and static they become, the more meaningless they are. You have an 'independent learning system'? Do you really mean that within the minimum of constraints the students can all the time choose what they are doing, how and when they do it? Are the relevant resources there and how do the students know they are relevant? Or do you mean that while the teachers determine overall what is to be learnt — and at times teach it — at other times the students are given a selection of individual assignments for which, hopefully, someone has checked that sufficient relevant information resources are available.

Or do you mean that . . . well, whatever you do mean the reality is likely to be much more complex than its labels imply. It isn't the label that matters if you are approaching 'resource-based learning' or 'individualised activities' or what-

ever you want to call it, it is the need to be alerted to the
facts that (a) any label is likely to be misleading, and (b) you
need to consider the problems that lie behind it if you want
your ideals to become reality.

To pursue the lighting analogy for a moment, by twitching
the wrong knob without thinking we can easily plunge the
student into total darkness, give him a very distorted or
unbalanced idea of what is going on, or create shadows in
which he cannot clearly see important pieces of the action.
On the other hand if we simply flood a bare stage with light
he may not know how to interpret the blank scene. So, to
sum up, in analogy terms we have been talking about ways of
producing different lighting plots but a lighting plot is only
there because it illuminates the characters and props in a play
(ie, it sets the scene for what is to happen). It is the play –
the educational process – that matters and the two are
complementary but if the setting is not right the play may
not be comprehended. This book is concentrating on
problems in that area of the process generally defined by
labels such as 'learning', 'individualised (work)', 'resource
intensive' as distinct from the conventional end of the
spectrum 'teaching', 'group (work)', 'person-intensive'. They
are bound to have specific implications for the playwright
and the producer, so to speak. In particular:

(a)   they bring a widening diversity of student activities –
      more and different at any given time
(b)   they must change to some degree the conventional role
      of the teacher as provider and controller
(c)   they require new or developed learning (work) skills in
      the student and may require the 'teacher' to transfer
      some of his own skills to the student.

This in turn means that you, the teacher contemplating
'resource-based learning' or whatever, must yourself look at
the educational situation from a slightly different angle –
that of the student. Whereas you used to decide not only
what was to be done, but how to do it, and how to judge the
results, now you may need to give the student more
independence of control – where you could previously be

the major information source you will have to ensure that alternative and relevant sources of information are available and that the student has the learning skills to make use of them.

In turn this means that we need to look in some depth at the following problems of design and manipulation in the educational process:

— goals — what the student may expect to achieve
— resource-oriented approaches and their implications — organisation — to help people find things out for themselves
— learner skills and capabilities — can the student use his learning 'tools'
— organising and managing the learning — guiding instead of controlling
— design and production of learning assignments and materials
— ways of monitoring and assessing individuals' work.

2. Goals

Ah yes, well now goals. Goals, objectives, end-products, call them what you will; they are a stumbling block for many teachers when they turn to resource-based work. Why should *I* bother with goals, they say:

'I know what I'm trying to do. . .why restrict oneself?'
'I can't possibly decide beforehand what my children are going to get out of it.'
'Objectives are so rigid, they don't allow any freedom to go off in new directions and one is always coming up against the problem of what to do when children don't achieve them.'
'Goals: yes I have them. I'm going to teach my children to do XYZ.'
'I can't see why they can't be led to *appreciate* Shakespeare.'

These remarks are commonplace and show the depth of feeling aroused by the emotive words 'goals' or 'objectives'. There is a lot of truth in them in some cases, in other cases they may just reflect an unwillingness to subject oneself to the discipline of what can be a fairly exacting mental analysis. Yet goals and all the objections to them need to be given serious attention because the nearer one gets to a resource *based* approach the more important goals become. A *teacher* may never have to define his aims overtly in terms of what individual children ought to achieve. He may know what content he wants to inculcate, he may well have developed methods of assessing if it has been achieved by at least some of his students, and a human being is still the most flexible instructing device there is. A teacher can pick up interesting leads, he can keep in his head where he is taking a group, he can carry out some form of comparative assessment, subjective though it may often be. But all this effectively pre-supposes a class group situation where the teacher can continually monitor his students' responses. The more one individualises work and the more student activities are diversified, the less possible it becomes. . . unless the 'teacher' has a lot of help built-in.

So what is a 'goal' or an 'objective' and why may it be important to have such things in resource-based or individualised work? Are the criticisms valid?

Well, basically a goal is what the word implies: it is something a learner can aim for – and if he can see what he is aiming for then he will know if he hits it. So a goal is a statement of intent as to *what the learner will be able to do when he has finished a particular piece of learning.* When you have read this chapter and undertaken the exercises in it you will, I hope, be able to:

(1) Define the terms 'goal' and 'behavioural objective'.
(2) Differentiate between a strictly behavioural objective and a more general goal.
(3) Identify when goals are stated in terms that show clearly what the learner has to aim for.
(4) Identify the major advantages and disadvantages of using goals in planning individual learning.

If you also complete the work assignments at the end of this chapter you should be able to write clear goals and behavioural objectives to cover specific learning aims.

Now, without going into too many semantic quibbles, we are using the word *goal* rather than *objective* because the latter has – even if not entirely accurately – come to be associated with the idea of behavioural objectives as put forward by Robert Mager. These are very clearly defined goals which specify *exactly* what the learner is going to be able to do: what tasks he will achieve, to what standards of performance and under what conditions. If you want an analogy the goal scorer is not just going to get a ball into the net; he is going, eight times out of ten, to put a round soccer ball into the right-hand corner of an undefended goal net by kicking the ball with either foot!

That, in itself, immediately highlights both the usefulness and the problems of using behavioural objectives. They can describe very accurately what should be achieved, but they have two big problems.

(1) They can be very trivial – and the more trivial a task the easier it is to identify it and to delude oneself about its

worth. We could have specified that our goal scorer should hit the ball every time into a 20-feet wide net from 3 feet away, with a very good chance of seeing him succeed — but unless we were trying to encourage a paraplegic it wouldn't be a very useful exercise! So you need to be careful that you are defining something worth learning.

(2) They can only meaningfully identify tasks that are capable of achievement. We couldn't realistically expect our scorer consistently to put the ball into the right-hand corner, etc, etc, if there was a good goalkeeper trying to stop him — so we have to take care that any behavioural objectives we write, because they are so specific, are realistic.

This has to be said since, whether they recognise it or not, it is *behavioural objectives* that worry most people: firstly because they appear to be restrictive in that their achievement implies keeping to a straight and narrow path of teaching; secondly because people feel that since objectives specify an exactly measurable performance by the learner they must restrict the *type* of learning. It has to be skills or knowledge capable of regurgitation because such cerebral activities as appreciation are not, it is said, quantifiable. In addition there is a feeling that the mere fact of setting an objective inevitably leads to failure since some children will probably not achieve it — and thereby 'fail'.

Let us dispose of this particular canard at once. It might happen in a class situation where the objective was inappropriate to the range of ability but we are concerned very much with individual and small group work where different objectives can be set for each person or group. . .so if we select unrealistic objectives it is our fault entirely.

In practice a behavioural objective is most useful when you want to define clearly what standards you want a student to achieve from a small piece of learning involving clearly testable skills and knowledge. A number of such objectives, strung together, may well in their turn be useful touchstones as to whether a broader goal is being achieved and if time is available it is useful for a teacher to build up such a cluster. Yet the more useful skill is likely to be that of defining broader goals — provided you feel that they are worthwhile.

Are they? Only you can decide so let us look at some of the objections cited at the beginning of this chapter.

'I have a goal; I'm going to teach my students (to do XYZ).' This justification always gets a lot of grumbles both from teachers — who feel that they *are* stating objectives — and from the educational theorists because they say that teachers are not defining what the *learner* should be able to do, they are merely stating their own aims. True and false: the teacher is more nearly right but not necessarily for the right reasons. Yes, you as a teacher are setting objectives or goals of a sort but what you are in effect doing is setting *your* objectives. If after your teaching the students appear to be doing what you have said they will, then *you* have achieved what you as a teacher set out to do. Now that may be fine for teaching although one might query how clearly you are defining your goals ('I'm teaching them history' for example is virtually meaningless). Nonetheless, in teaching, the teacher is in control of what he wants to achieve and if, for good or bad reasons, he turns a blind eye when some students cannot do what he wants, or he makes his goals more elastic to accommodate problems that arise . . . or he throws them right out of the window to pursue something else that comes up in the middle of a lesson . . . that is his decision because he is in a position to control what is going on in a group.

If, however, you, as teacher, move over even to resource-oriented and individualised teaching then such control becomes less easy because you have in effect had to formalise — perhaps even fossilise — your teaching content and put it in a form that individuals can use: the advantages of individual variations in pace and level are balanced by a diminution of flexibility and a difficulty in reacting quickly. It becomes more necessary to be able to find out how different individuals are progressing and that in turn implies knowing what *they* rather than you are aiming at.

So, the more you move towards resource-based work, and especially toward individualised *learning* where the student makes more of his own decisions, the less valid a simple statement of teaching aims becomes. When you get into the situation where a collection of students is working even partly independently on a variety of tasks at the same time, then the direct overall control of the teacher is minimal. If your time is not to be grossly over-loaded, the tasks and learning materials given to the students have to be at least partially structured so that they can work for spells without your attention − and structuring implies that goals and, if appropriate, specific objectives have been worked out from the learner's point of view: not 'I (the teacher) am teaching them to . . . ' but 'I (the learner) am going to be able to do X'. Students working on their own need reassurance that they are progressing and it is very difficult to give them this if you do not know where they are heading.

Much the same arguments apply to the objection 'I know what I'm trying to do . . . why restrict myself?'

You may know what you are trying to do and be able to control it while you are *teaching* a single class or even two or three fair-sized groups. Once you are dealing with individuals using not just your knowledge but a wide variety of resource items and activities then it gets very difficult to remember, in the increasing spread of activities, just who has done what; it is even more difficult to control it. Identifiable goals of some description then become a very useful tool in the task of judging what progress is being made by each student and of identifying where help needs to be given.

In the same way you are not inevitably 'restricting' either yourself or the student in defining an overall goal for a particular assignment. It is not as fixed as the laws of the Medes and the Persians. You can always create additional goals if it seems appropriate or change the ones you have already decided on, or, if you don't want to dictate, you can agree goals with the student. What you are doing in either case is clarifying a situation in such a way that you can always see what is going on.

So? All right, but what about the argument that goals and objectives are useful only for facts or practical skills. You cannot surely define artistic or emotional outcomes; if you try to define 'appreciation' or what goes into an opinion are you not simply going to restrict the student to your viewpoint?

Whether that argument is valid is dubious — if you as the teacher cannot clarify what you mean by a word like 'appreciate' or 'enjoy' one could well query if you know what you are doing. Yet the problem cannot be ignored because a lot of our scepticism comes from a worry as to whether, by defining abstract concepts, we may destroy the very thing we are hoping to achieve. Again it is important to examine this very real worry and to spot that this is one instance when behavioural objectives might be inappropriate while more general goals may not. How are you going to tell if a student has 'enjoyed' a book or, say, formed his own opinion about some historical event unless there is some recognisable way in which he can show you how he has done? In individual work, especially, the student certainly needs the knowledge of how he is getting on in order to reinforce his motivation and his confidence in his own learning skills since he does not have the opportunity of feedback that he would have in a class. If what he is doing does not have a visible outcome then he must get his feedback from you and therefore you must know what to check. The point here about general goals is that you need to make them appropriate. He doesn't need to state an opinion pre-ordained for him; the goal you can set for, say, enjoying a book might be a simple set of indications. Does he talk about the book after he has read it? Does he want to read further books by the same author? Does he evince complete uninterest if the book is discussed? If he does show signs of enjoyment then you can reinforce his 'success' or take other action; if not, you are alerted to a 'failure' and the need to do something. You can in fact define a number of criteria which may enable you to judge whether the student has achieved what you hoped without making them force him into any particular line of thought. Indeed most of the objections to goals as being constricting are based on two misconceptions.

(1)   The basic mistake people make is to assume that defining a goal makes it automatically restrictive so far

as the learning is concerned — ie, it dictates what is to be done. What they overlook is that a goal or an objective is just a statement of a desired result, an end product. It simply says what a learner will be able to do *when* he has reached it. It doesn't say *how* the learning has to be achieved and its presence doesn't stop the learner deviating on the way: it just tries to identify how he and you can find out when you have reached your destination. You as the teacher may decide you want the student to learn in a certain way; you as the teacher may decide that, because of shortage of time, or student ability or any other factor, you are going to set a restricted goal for your student to aim at but that is your teaching decision, not one dictated by goals as such. After all, you are designing the learning; you can, if you want to, just give your student a goal to aim at, pat him on the head and tell him to come back in a week's time. If he has enough initiative, relevant learning skills and necessary physical resources, he may get there and be free to explore all sorts of avenues along the route. Then again he may not be able to do it and you may feel you have to provide him with guidance or even direction. That is again *your teaching decision* based on your knowledge of the student and the circumstances. Do it but don't blame the goal statement for any restrictions *you* put on the student's methods of learning or on his freedom to deviate.

(2) The other mistake is really overzealousness by converts! People — and that includes teachers of objectives — misuse goals and in particular behavioural objectives. They assume the strict behavioural objective is universally applicable when really it is useful mainly for defining small pieces of learning. For the teacher it is a specific tool to help in planning a single lesson or a small work assignment where the outcome can be clearly seen. The error is to try to fix precise standards and conditions where perhaps a more general statement of intent would be better; and then, of course, people rebel.

All of these arguments bring us to the clinching argument for not defining your *goals.*

'I can't possibly decide what my children are going to get out of it.'

No? Well, you probably *can* if you try: what you mean is that you don't want to because (a) you don't feel you have the right to do so or (b) you find it too much effort and trouble because the outcomes are likely to be many and various.

Let us disregard the second although noting that we all suffer from it at times; one of the problems of adopting a resource-based or individualised approach is that it makes many more demands on the teacher.

You may, then, feel that you don't have the right to dictate your students' learning. That, as a general policy, is clearly your decision though I suspect that most of us do not really mean even that. We want to imply that we do not wish to

(i) make everyone learn a particular skill, etc, at a particular time even though the skill or piece of knowledge may be essential — we want the student to be able to acquire it when he needs it or when his interest is aroused

(ii) trammel lines of inquiry: 'how one learns is more important than what one learns'

(iii) stop students from chasing off after something which has taken their interest but is unrelated to the ostensible goal.

The irony is that the more one argues along these lines the more a resource-based and individualised approach is likely to be necessary and the more need there is for identifying some goals so that relevant work can be provided when it is needed. The idea that once you define a goal or an objective you are necessarily forcing a student along a predetermined learning path applies only to formal teaching situations. It is worth reiterating that a goal or a behavioural objective is simply a definition of a learning target that can be reached. It does not by itself define either *when* or *how* it should be achieved but it does enable you to design materials or assignments which you can use to help a child *when he is ready*; it doesn't have to be issued to everyone at the same time. It may enable you to produce different pieces of material at different levels and degrees of help for different students. You are not dictating what students learn by form- ulating goals; you are simply defining outcomes which you feel are desirable or useful for them to achieve at some point. Whether they all eventually reach the goals depends on their abilities and on your decisions. Goals do not even have to be formulated by you, since it is quite possible for a teacher and student to agree a goal in discussion.

So let us look more closely at *goals* because it is quite true that a danger of thinking solely about objectives is that they do inhibit many people; even some of their proponents tend not to be able to see the wood for the trees and to continue that analogy, it is no good selecting and chopping down a single tree if you cannot spot the path you are supposed to be clearing.

Now, the difference between a goal and a behavioural objective is not *just* one of degree, it is one of definition. If a behavioural objective describes exactly what a learner will be expected to be able to do when he has learnt something, then by definition it has got to be describing something fairly small and precise. A *goal* is usually a more general intent expressed in terms of performance but only with sufficient indications of that performance to enable (a) the student to see what he has to aim at, and (b) both of you to judge whether in general it has been achieved.

Thus a goal is often just a statement of general achieve- ment (eg, 'will be able to distinguish between a goal and an objective') which does not specifically lay down standards; you can negotiate those with individual learners who thus can have their own differential objectives to aim at within the overall goal. Yet this very broadness has its own dangers since it is easy to produce what Mager and others have called 'fuzzies' — an apt word for a definition which sounds impressive but which becomes elusive as soon as you look at it closely. Like an objective, a goal should be unambiguous in general terms to both the setter and the learner who is going to have to try to achieve it. The acid test is whether the descriptive words or phrases would be clear to the learner.

Which of these would you think of as 'fuzzy'? The student will be able to:

(1)   speak French fluently
(2)   add three numbers correctly
(3)   appreciate a particular poem.

(1)   'Speak French fluently' — a non-fuzzy goal you would say; but is it? 'Speak French' — yes that is an observable phenomenon: 'fluently' is the crunch. It sounds excellent. We all know what fluently means — to speak like a native. Hmm . . . have you ever heard some Frenchmen speaking their own language or — let's not have discrimination — some English speaking English: slurred sounds, colloquial short-cuts, broad regional accents almost incomprehensible to people outside the region . . . So that is not much clearer. What about: 'To speak French without an accent that makes it difficult for others to comprehend you, without making grammatical mistakes, and using recognised idioms of the country'. Is that what we mean? Well at least it is something that you can judge because both you and the learner can see what it means. If you are not worried about accent you can say so. . . The point is that you have isolated the important components and you can come to an agreement. The learner can't talk without making grammatical mistakes? . . . so you can adjust both goals and any detailed objectives to suit.

(2)   'Add three numbers correctly.' Well, as a goal it is clear enough. You can both see what is involved and the learner can demonstrate to you both that it has been achieved. It is also a fair base for constructing a set of objectives to suit the different students; your bright ones may be brought to add *any* three numbers correctly *all the time*; some may only be able to add single digit numbers with occasional mistakes but those

are personal objectives and goals you can agree with the people concerned. The overall goal gives you scope in individual work while providing a general performance to aim at.

(3) Appreciate a particular poem! Ha! clearly a fuzzy but one which any fiddling of semantics won't make any clearer. You cannot define 'appreciate'!

No, maybe you cannot in so many words but that need not stop you providing an observable goal in terms of performance that indicates to you whether success has been achieved even if the student can't be sure. Would you accept one or more of the following as evidence of 'appreciation'?

— He is inspired to try to write a poem in the same vein.
— He will of his own free will come and talk about the poem.
— If the matter is raised he will be prepared willingly to discuss the poem and his reactions to it.
— He wants to read more poems by the same writer or on similar subjects.

And would you, equally, agree that absence of all of these signs should make *you* think again about your teaching?

Note that a goal may be one that you can only *observe* in terms of a student's performance and you may not be able to discuss it with him in advance for fear of invalidating it as a touchstone by which you can judge success. This does not mean that it is not worth doing. In resource-based work especially, you need to find out if the resources are working and in any case you may not wish to make all the goals known to your students in advance. Do you or don't you tell the learner what he is expected to achieve? There's no clear rule and it is up to you — the only guideline is that the more he has to work on his own the more he will need some guidance as to where he is going and how he is doing, either in terms of success he can see for himself or in terms of reassurance and feedback from you.

So much for goals. We have considered them at length because you are unlikely to get very far in using resource-based approaches unless you have got your own reasons —

and that means your goals – clear.

This chapter has, hopefully, defined goals in general and discussed why they are likely to be needed. It has not taught you to write goals in detail but if you want to learn that skill the reading assignments on the following pages should help you. In any case you might like to remember the following facts:

(1)   GOALS and OBJECTIVES are both simply statements of expected outcomes. They do not restrict *content*, learning/teaching method or, indeed inhibit changes of direction of themselves. Only you do that.

(2)   A GOAL is a general statement of intent identified by performance of the learner. It may be a task *he* can identify as a measure of achievement or a statement of behaviour *you* can observe which will tell you something about whether the goal has been achieved.

(3)   You can think of a GOAL as a target: some students may hit the bull's-eye, some only get an 'outer'. It is your decision whether you tell them the difference, or whether indeed you set different individual standards for each learner – BUT you can't decide that if you haven't defined the goal in advance.

(4)   BEHAVIOURAL OBJECTIVES define much more precisely what part of a goal should be attained and in what manner. They are important, useful for measuring achievement of specific learning operations.

Lastly remember: defining goals and objectives is useful *but* they are not a be-all-and-end-all as some protagonists like to urge. Someone operating a fruit machine has his goal – and even his objective – of obtaining money by getting certain combinations of symbols. To know that doesn't help him very much in achieving it. Nor does it guarantee that it is a valid goal to have! Don't just state the goal and leave the student operating the fruit machine of chance. The goal is only the first step in individualising learning and does not absolve you from thinking out the various ways a student may achieve it, or from providing the means for him to do so.

Suggested reading assignment on objectives

1. Two very useful primers on defining goals and objectives are:

Stating behavioural objectives for classroom instruction (N E Gronlund)

Preparing instructional objectives (R F Mager)

Details of both will be found in the information index at the end of this book. If you wish to explore further the problems of producing objectives we suggest that you read both of them and carry out the exercises they suggest. We advise you to use the revised (1975) edition of Mager.

2. You will note that the writers take apparently differing views on the *terms* in which objectives should be stated and on what elements should be included in them. You may find it useful to compare Mager's approach throughout his book with Gronlund's ideals in his Chapters 1 (especially pp 4–6), 2 and 3 and then to consider the following questions.

  (i) To what extent do their attitudes to general conceptual terms like 'understand' differ in practice?

 (ii) How does Gronlund attempt to clarify such terms? and How would you expect Mager to do the same?

(iii) Where, if anywhere, do you feel that Mager's insistence on the inclusion of standards of achievement might be appropriate and where might it be inappropriate?

As an experiment you might like to consider how, for example, you could assess Gronlund's suggested student activity 'listens with attention'.

3. It is difficult to give you feedback on this assignment. Fortunately both books contain a considerable degree of built-in feedback and if you carry out their exercises and those given below you should be fully alerted to the problems and advantages of objective design.

Suggested post-reading activities

(a) Produce one or more *general goals* relevant to your own teaching situation. Use the checklist in Appendix A of Gronlund to assess their effectiveness.

(b) Produce, from one of your general goals, one or more *specific learning objectives.* Look at Appendix B of Gronlund. Do the verbs used in your specific objectives correspond with the ones he suggests? If you are writing behavioural objectives, do they contain Mager's three basic elements? If not, why not? What are your reasons?

3. Teaching and the resource-oriented approach

'We've got resource-based learning. The head has developed a resource centre and we use it for individual work; all the first-year maths is on worksheets.'

Once again the labels take charge. There is an almost universal assumption that 'resource-based' or 'individualised' work must almost inevitably be 'learning' rather than 'teaching' as well, but is this so – and is it desirable in any case?

Well, as various public personalities have so truly said from time to time, 'It all depends on what you mean by . . . '. Let us look at the various ways in which an educational situation, as defined by our four dimensions, can be organised. In the following notes I have taken the word assignment to mean a piece of work allotted to a student, but left basically for him to complete rather than his being taken through it with constant participation by the teacher.

The main ways of organising an educational situation at any time are:

lecturing

group teaching

seminar (group discussion usually led by a teacher)

tutorial

group assignments
– controlled
– guided
– largely independent

individual/pair assignments
– largely independent
– guided
– controlled

'accidental learning'

The last is quite often cited as desirable. 'It doesn't matter what they learn but how they learn'; 'the most valuable bits of learning are those which are not planned' . . . , etc. So it may be; but it is clearly very dangerous to *depend on it* and by definition one cannot prepare for it except by flooding the situation with stimulus materials, so we need not consider it here. The others are quite sufficient since they are the major formal ways of trying to ensure that student knowledge, experience and skills are systematically developed.

Now it is worth noting that in the first four of these activities a teacher is necessarily directly involved and in all the others he has a part to play even if he writes himself out of direct contact by providing assignments, instructions or other indirect guidance. Even in so-called independent learning at least some general goals are likely to have been agreed with the 'teacher'.

The important point is that it is the extent of the teacher's influence that really determines whether the result is teaching (classified as the activity having a didactic element), learning or a mixture of the two — as most often happens. Numbers as such do not determine whether an activity is teaching or learning. Thus a tutorial is the prime example of individualised educational activity but the usual tutorial is a teaching activity. Only if it is initiated by the learner using the 'teacher' just as a resource does it move toward *learning as an activity*. An individual work assignment can give a student scope for his own inquiry (learning) or it can virtually tell him what to do and how to do it (teaching). In the same way groups may be working under their own initiative and impulsion or under the guidance or direction of a teacher. So many such activities combine elements of both teaching and learning.

In the same way one cannot say that because work is resource-oriented it is necessarily going to be a learning rather than a teaching activity. Once again the labels are misleading since most resource-oriented strategies centre round the 'middle' of the range, 'person assisted by resources' or 'resources assisted by person' rather than being genuinely resource-based — even if their protagonists use the 'resource-based' label. There are probably three basic approaches.

The *'teacher as resource'* approach which most of us use is, agreed, really a 'teaching' approach though a lot of teachers still try to use it when individualising work. The problem then is twofold: you have somehow to split your time up so that any student can always tap your expertise – and the more you diversify learning activities the more difficult and frustrating for the learner that becomes; and you have to be a fountain of knowledge. That may be possible at low learner-knowledge levels (eg, with young children) but the more knowledgeable the students become the harder the task we are imposing on the teachers.

The *resource-based* approach at the other extreme is admittedly basically linked to *learning*. 'Aha,' you say, 'I told you so'; but do you realise just what the concept 'resource-based' really means? It implies not just that the teacher is using resources to help him but that the student's work is literally based on learning from resources of various kinds. The teacher has to move sideways to become, as so many people glibly assert, just another resource, one among many. What comparatively few people do is to face up to the real practical consequences of this approach which needs not only a massive and well organised collection of information and tools but also new skills of organisation on the part of the teacher. What most of us do when 'teacher as resource' becomes unviable is to drift into some variant of the middle way.

We might call this the *'resource assisted'* approach and its essential characteristics are that the teacher is still a major source of information and guidance but tries to 'extend' himself by such activities as:

(a) Preparing work in advance that, so to speak, formalises his teaching on paper – much so-called worksheet learning is of this type where the producer/teacher is effectively saying, 'I cannot attend to everyone at once but by codifying my teaching I can give myself time to help those who really need it'. As an advantage he can perhaps also formalise his teaching at several levels of difficulty to cope with different student abilities.

(b) Providing a variety of content by using items, especially physical resources, which he knows or *guesses* to be in the vicinity: 'You want to do something on ships, dear.

Well, go and look in the library'.

(c) Designing differing 'assignments' with or without
     additional materials, to enable various students — or
     types of student — to carry out certain tasks or to
     achieve specified ends (eg, a workcard which helps a
     student get information from a particular book).

It is a useful and convenient approach because it can solve
the problem of availability of knowledge, and can help to
cope with different individuals. Yet it can also easily get the
worst of both worlds. What if there isn't anything appropriate on 'ships' in the library? Or what if the codified
'worksheets' are so arid and similar that the students get sick
of them where they might have enjoyed the live teaching?
These points we must take up later on. Suffice at present that
all the 'middle' choices can again be used for teaching (as in
(a) above for example) or for learning. They do not by
themselves imply one or the other.

On the other hand your decisions on how much you want
to influence the work determine whether you are aiming
towards teaching or learning, in that they define the extent
to which the student or teacher will influence work and
hence the proportion of didacticism that will be included.
Here it is true that the more control you want the student to
have over his work the more you are likely to individualise it
so that it becomes particular to him and the more likely you
are to need a resource-oriented approach, because the more
options he has, the wider the range of information, etc, he
may possibly require. Then, too, the more you want overtly
or tacitly to have control over the student's work the more
likely you are to think of a group, of using a common set of
information as content instead of letting students use a
variety of sources, of teaching rather than, even, guiding.
None the less the point remains that you can if you wish still
individualise work and make it dependent on use of a variety
of physical resources while still retaining complete control
over what is to be learnt and even how it is to be learnt. In
that case the didactic element is obviously strong and if we
are honest we are still *teaching* though in a different way.
There is nothing intrinsically wrong in this unless you are

philosophically opposed to teaching. I'm not trying to put forward any particular approach as ideal; all would seem to have their uses in the appropriate place and may even be used in combination within a single educational situation.

What I am trying to do is to make clear that in designing assignments, planning, etc, in deciding whether to embark on 'resource-oriented', 'individualised work' approaches or not, you should look at the realities not the labels. If you can identify what you feel is most important in terms of one or more of our 'dimensions' and then read off the consequences and use the information you have a better chance of bringing success in learning to your students — and that, surely, is why we are all in business.

If you want to explore the problem further in your own case you might like to carry out the small exercise at the end of this chapter. It has been designed so that you can do it either by yourself or as a group discussion exercise with others.

A critical checklist for determining the control pattern in learning and teaching situations

Introduction

An instructional situation is defined by who controls the various aspects. Does the *teacher* do so, or the learner, or do they genuinely cooperate? By selecting one (or more) items from each group you can build up a 'picture' of the situation. You might like to apply the following questions to a teaching or learning situation of your own.

Definitions

Are you talking about a situation where:

A. GOALS
   (1) are all determined by the teacher?
   (2) are determined overall by the teacher but in detail by the learner?
   (3) are agreed between teacher and learner?
   (4) are determined by the learner to suit himself?
   (5) there are no overt goals?

B. CONTENT
   (6) is determined entirely by the teacher?
   (7) is determined by the teacher in outline but by the learner in detail?
   (8) is determined by the teacher and learner in combination (within any goal constraints)?
   (9) is determined entirely by the learner?

C. METHODS OF LEARNING
   (10) are determined entirely by the teacher?
   (11) are determined in outline by the teacher but in detail by the learner?
   (12) are determined by agreement between the teacher and learner?
   (13) are determined entirely by the learner?

D. METHODS OF ASSESSING
(14) are determined entirely by the teacher?
(15) are determined by the teacher and the learner in agreement?
(16) are determined largely by the learner but monitored by the teacher?
(17) are determined largely by the learner and not monitored?

E. OUTSIDE CONSTRAINTS (time, curriculum, etc)
(18) are controlled by the teacher?
(19) are controlled wholly or partly by outside forces?
(20) are controlled by the teacher and learner together?
(21) are controlled by the learner?

Note down your selections either as a set of numbers or a group of sentences. Then read on.

This list is intended simply as a self-critical tool to help you define for yourself what you actually are intending to do. It does not suggest that any one approach is 'better', but does show up elements likely to be incompatible.

In general if your 'survey' produced a list of broadly parallel factors (say 1, 7, 11, 14) then you probably have a consistent approach and a basis for working. If on the other hand you found, say, 2, 9, 13, 14 then something is awry, for teacher and learner will be in conflict over what they expect to happen. Certainly the higher numbered patterns in each group (eg, 4, 5, 12, 13) cannot realistically be used if 19 is also applicable.

You can use the list as a check on your general design of any given learning situation or activity — particularly to find out where something may be going wrong.

It is important for this reason to identify the control factors operating on any given teaching or learning situation.

1. If the factors are incompatible with each other (eg, if you claim 9 but also try to implement 14) then you are likely to have a very hit-and-miss situation, students may be confused and it may be difficult to identify what is going wrong.

2. You may not, in reality, be doing what you fondly think you are doing! (It is for example common to find people talking of doing resource-based learning but identifying factors 1, 6, 11 and 14 as being aspects of what they are involved in.)

4. The teacher's role in resource-oriented work

If you are still intending, after all that, to explore seriously the resource-oriented and individualised approaches then it is time to consider your own role, because the teacher's role is likely to change drastically. To take an analogy, you will no longer be the driver of a conducted tour taking thirty or so clients over a predetermined route. You must become much more of a cross between a travel agent and a universal uncle, organising a wide variety of tours on which your students can go. Your role changes to that of offering guidance, of answering queries, of rescuing those who get into trouble, as has been pointed out by so many enthusiasts for resource-based work. What has not so often been pointed out is that your actual travel agent/uncle, to be successful, has to know what he is doing in the first place; if he recommends a route to someone he must be sure there is a reasonable chance of the client enjoying it; if he offers a package deal it should fulfil expectations.

That in turn means that, since you have less control over what goes on you need, to continue the analogy, to have studied in advance the likely learning country and if necessary made discreet arrangements to further your clients' progress. You will have found interesting places and made sure relevant information about them is available in the right language at the right time, you will have provided maps so that clients can find their way around; you will have spotted places where clients might run into difficulties and decided what can be done to help. This is not to say you will obliterate the difficulty but you will identify possible ways for people to solve the problems and their implications. In our learning country there may be a river to be crossed. You can find or provide a bridge, so that there is no problem — but then the student may not learn how to cross rivers; you can check there is a boat — but can he row? You should find out; you can just tell him of the difficulty if you feel he can surmount it on his own — but you have of course checked that he can swim? In each case different skills and con-sequences are involved and unless you believe in leaving everything to chance it is your responsibility to ensure that the individual has the capabilities you 'think' he has or that an answer is provided. There is nothing like drowning to put a client off individual exploration for good!

A change to 'resource' and 'individual' oriented work, therefore, means a need for a fresh look at the skills needed by both teacher and pupil. In an ordinary teaching situation it is fair to say that deficiencies in a student's learning skills can often be overcome but in an individual situation where the onus is on him to progress, they become very important. You might like to try and jot down the main ones you feel a student needs, before you continue.

The main problem most of us find in doing this exercise is to avoid putting down vague thoughts like: 'ability to find out things'. That is not really an identifiable skill but the result of a collection of skills. The sort of skills to identify are:

Basic
— recognise signals, cues, etc
— use classroom equipment
Information extraction
— extract information, showing grasp of meaning
— synthesise information from several sources
— assess and interpret information for relevance and accuracy
— present information in various forms
Practical
— carry out tasks from instructions
— carry out tasks from acquired knowledge
— solve problems from given information
— solve problems needing 'new' information

You may be able to identify others but these are essential — and we very often blithely assume that the students already have them — hence the acres of slavish copying from encyclopedias that decorate many school walls in the name of 'finding out', and the repetitive worksheets that really only teach tricks of answering, not understanding of a process.

If there is no evidence of understanding or discrimination then, unless we have checked beforehand and are sure the student does have the skills, bad work of this kind is *our* fault not his — but that is no consolation to a student who has learnt little and may not even be aware of it. Clearly the student's learning skills will need developing and this will raise other problems of why particular assignments are produced and what forms they take. It also raises the problem of your own skills, for much of what a student does you may have had to do beforehand. What particular skills are *you* likely to need to bring into play?

Can you for example define goals (and if possible objectives) clearly? Even if you consider these as only applicable to certain learning tasks they will be needed at some time.

You might like, as before, to think of what skills you are likely to need.

What about:

(1) ability to identify problem areas in particular pieces of work you set? (This means, in effect, being able to find out what is involved in reaching particular goals.)

(2) ability to organise the work of a large number of individuals at the same time? Have you:
   (i) means of keeping trace of what each one is doing
   (ii) means of monitoring progress when important areas of learning are concerned
   (iii) the skill to choose the right sequence of work for any particular student?

You will also need to be able to identify and provide appropriate work activities to enable students to reach particular goals, to establish whether there are any good reasons why these activities should be individual, small group, etc, and to make sure that any combination of activities is motivating. If you are *teaching* you can vary your presentation and level of difficulty immediately if you spot the students getting bored or obviously failing to comprehend. Prefabricated individual work assignments are by their very nature less flexible in responding to such problems unless you are constantly supervising their performance — and that defeats the object of the exercise. It is easy, too, to string together a series of such assignments of which each one is adequate by itself but which in combination bore the pants off the students carrying them out. Repetitiveness, lack of 'people pattern' variety, increasing teacher-direction are all common features of individualised work once the first flush of enthusiasm has worn off for the producer. It is therefore very important to be able to identify the purpose of the activity — which means again referring to the goals — and then to select from the different types of activity available one which will (a) achieve its purpose and (b) if possible give planned variety for the student.

But this, of course, is not all. The big change in role is from being a director to being a manager. Identification of goals, the skills that will be needed and the appropriate types of activities may help you to design various work assignments, both individual and group, for your students. What, however, are you going to do with the assignments once you have them? You are constantly going to be faced with decisions on how to organise: (a) the content of the work, (b) the work load and pattern of work, (c) the environment in which the work is being done.

For instance, are you going to keep overall control of the content? Is everyone working more or less towards the same goal? If they are, then are they all doing variations on the same task or are you going to arrange matters so that they have a choice of routes, perhaps through a morass of assignments (as an example, are you producing a sequence of worksheets, or setting a project goal but letting the students choose their own ways of tackling it)? If you are letting your students determine the content of their work how are you monitoring what they achieve?

Again, is the work going, for a given period of time, to be purely individual or will it include specified times when groups get together? What effects will your decisions have on timetabling problems, on continuity of learning, on the different speeds at which individuals work?

Or, again, can you organise the environment so that the students can do what you want them to? Will they have to reorganise furniture, bring in resources or go outside the school? Will they suddenly have to break off in the middle of an assignment to go to French or games?

These decisions and all the others like them become more and more frequent the further you move from formal teaching where the same decisions will serve for a whole group. Even in the easiest situation where you simply 'individualise' a set piece of teaching for a class by turning the teaching into worksheet form, the variables start multiplying rapidly. All sorts of problems immediately arise even by simply allowing for a minimum flexibility in level of difficulty so that students who find one part hard can be diverted to an easier method or vice versa and by ensuring that students complete each stage (and some thus take longer than planned, some less time). Thus one student is in trouble even with the most 'basic' level and is steadily falling behind. A second student finds some work too easy, so tries and succeeds with a harder worksheet, but runs into trouble with the next stage and has to backtrack. For a third student even the hardest level is clearly very easy.

Now in one way each of those students is being catered for better than in the formal teaching situation where student One might have been completely lost by the third week, while student Three might well be bored to tears. On the other hand you are already being faced with decisions — what to do about the student who is clearly not going to finish the complete task? What about the one who will be finished by half-term? You picked up student Two's problem but have you missed any others? Clearly this situation, even if the activities are appropriate, causes several problems. Should all students complete all the work? If so you may have to teach the poorer ones or make it simpler.

Let us have a look at another situation, where you are giving students much more freedom of choice, say in a project. Here our learning country analogy becomes even more apposite since you are in effect showing your pupils a piece of, to them, unexplored learning and saying 'see you on the other side', something which is far too often done. Then you need to have surveyed the project yourself in advance to see if all your students are skilled enough to do it — and if not, have arranged to help them improve their skills. Even so you may need to produce guidelines, booklets of tips, etc. The problems have changed in that you are not producing massive sets of work material but organising existing materials and tools so they are available at the right time and at the right level. At the same time you have still got to consider the speed and variations in ability of each pupil and because you have less 'control' it is more difficult. You may end up producing only a small amount of support material but your means of keeping tabs on your clients may need to be vastly more elaborate.

What level of achievement do you expect in people crossing your learning country?

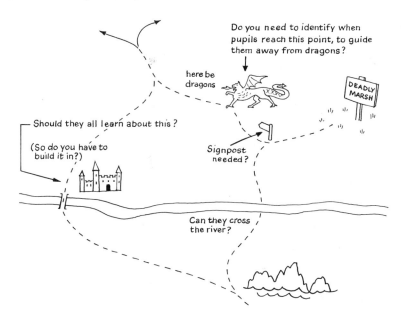

And these, remember are comparatively 'easy' situations. If you extend them to allow your students to take widely differing routes toward even the same goal, or if, on the tourist analogy, you are simply going to turn them loose to wander across country as they choose, then your decisions really become important if your students are going to learn with any certainty. If external factors such as limited time start creeping in, then you have even more considerations to take into account and they may well determine how you *can* reorganise the work.

You then have to think of your role on two levels.

(a) Problems of organising the educational situation in general — for example your decisions on planning a particular area of learning or what to do during a particular period of time (roughly equivalent to a 'scheme of work' in formal teaching).

(b) Problems of producing and organising single assignments or series of assignments to enable students to reach specific goals which you have decided, or agreed, should be attained within the overall plan.

Both of these which are organisational activities also involve the implementation of your plans, the problem of ensuring that the content of the learning is absorbed and used by the students. It all emphasises the change of role from teaching to managing.

All these problems are very closely connected and in practice it is rarely possible to do exactly what you would like; external influences such as the headmaster or lack of time will keep interfering. It may be worth, therefore, looking at the factors which determine the shape of any generalised educational plan and seeing what their collective effects are likely to be. By considering them you can often tell whether what you want to do is possible or, if not, what your next best line of approach is. Page 51 shows the major variables and if you can identify them in detail for any particular situation you are half way to being able to decide how to organise it.

The point to remember is that an interpretation of these factors is not 'restrictive' any more than goals are 'restrictive' by themselves. It describes the possible options for any given set of factors. In other words you are not saying 'in weeks 1—5 all the students are going to have to do X, so . . . .'.

What you are saying is: 'This is what needs to be learnt (goals) and for these reasons (exams? skills needed to achieve something else? pleasure?). Right, now how would I like this to be done . . .?' Then you can say, 'Well, that's how I'd like it to be. What about the other factors? Can the students cope with it? Have I got the resources? Can I handle it like this?'

When you have established these points then you can design your overall plan and see exactly what it implies in terms of implementation — the detailed student activities for various parts of the work, any new assignments or materials you need. But it is just a framework in which learning can take place and frameworks can be modified if needed, or even rebuilt if they prove unsatisfactory.

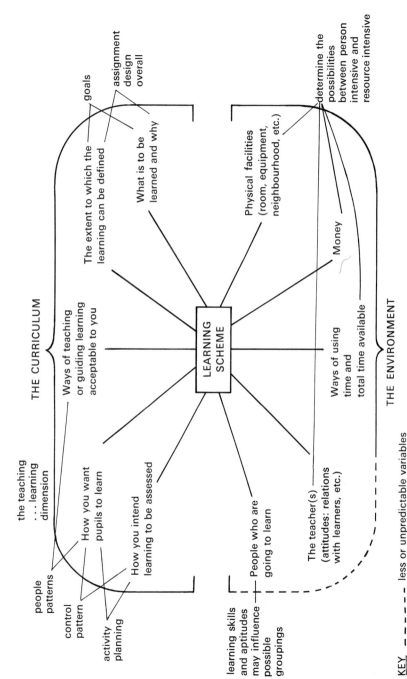

THE CURRICULUM

the teaching
... learning
dimension

people
patterns

control
pattern

activity
planning

Ways of teaching
or guiding learning
acceptable to you

How you want
pupils to learn

How you intend
learning to be assessed

The extent to which the
learning can be defined

goals

assignment
design
overall

What is to be
learned and why

LEARNING
SCHEME

Physical facilities
(room, equipment,
neighbourhood, etc.)

Money

determine the
possibilities
between person
intensive and
resource intensive

Ways of using
time and
total time available

The teacher(s)
(attitudes: relations
with learners, etc.)

People who are
going to learn

learning skills
and aptitudes
may influence
possible
groupings

THE ENVIRONMENT

KEY - - - - - less or unpredictable variables

You may, for example, find you are in a position to say: 'During the next half-term we are going to be dealing with this subject area. I shall want all my students to reach goals X, Y and Z but apart from that I can give them freedom. Now we don't have much information in the library. Shall I get some and organise it, or shall I write my own materials?' Or, you might have to say: 'In six weeks' time as many students as possible are going to need to do ABCD because of an external examination. They are fairly similar in ability and there is a lot of ground to cover. Do I teach them direct, or prepare individualised worksheets? . . .'

Your final decisions come from what your examination of all the factors leads you to believe is possible — in terms of teaching/learning and of preparation. In the same way your decisions at the level of designing particular student assignments are, consciously or unconsciously, governed by the set of variables described by our four dimensions. If you can consciously identify them and determine the effects of various combinations you have a better chance of producing assignments and materials that will enable your students to succeed. (See Chs. 6,8) The essential characteristic of any resource-oriented, individualised approach is that it works only if the conditions are right and the ground work has been efficiently carried out by the teacher. After all, even if you give your students complete freedom of choice, you cannot abrogate *your* responsibility. Because the learning is individualised and you cannot really split yourself into 20 or more parts simultaneously, other means have to be found of ensuring that relevant information and tools are available to help students achieve their goals and that guidance is provided where necessary. Hence you will need to be concerned with

— determining relevant student activities and assignments
— organising physical resources both for retrieval and for usefulness
— producing or modifying items of learning material
— organising the learning environment so that learning is facilitated
— monitoring and assessing students' progress.

The second part of this book is concerned entirely with the practical problems of acquiring skills needed by a change of emphasis to 'resource-oriented' and 'individualised' work, and by the consequent change in the teacher's role.

5. Planning learning activities and assignments

At the end of Chapter 4, we agreed that the teacher tending towards individualising learning must consider his role on two levels.

(a) The general level of managing the whole situation.

(b) The more localised level of producing appropriate work and guidelines for his students to undertake — in other words designing the individual or group assignments they will be expected to carry out.

This second task may well be the most important part of preparing for individualised learning since the assignment(s) and the materials associated with them are the product with which the student will come most immediately into contact — just as the actual lesson is the product of teaching with which he comes immediately into contact; the organisation of his wider environment he may well take for granted without realising the work that has gone into it!

Hence we are faced with the problem of designing assignments to suit individuals or small collaborative groups rather than designing lessons to suit a class group. There is, however, a problem of definition which we may as well sort out. No one has yet agreed universally on what is the word to describe the individual learning equivalent of a teaching *lesson*. Learning 'opportunities', 'activities', 'experiences', 'assignments' are all words used apparently indiscriminately. For clarity's sake we will suggest there is a difference. An opportunity is simply a realisable chance for a student to achieve something provided he grasps it; it does not define *how* he grasps it. That is the function of an activity, which is something a student does (eg, finds out) which enables him, in conjunction with any *information content*, to experience something or to develop his knowledge. An assignment is the product — the instructions or guidance — that will help him.

In practice then, a learning assignment is a piece of work designed to combine and translate into practical terms a number of activities to provide *experiences, gains in knowledge*, and, hence, formation and development of concepts and skills, attitudes, etc. It may simply be an outline set of guides for carrying out specific tasks or it may incorporate resource material of various kinds.

In itself the production of such an assignment creates or allows the development of opportunities in the true sense of realisable chances for the learner to achieve something he can identify. One may argue that opportunities occur naturally; so they do but it is a fallacy to assume that all students will necessarily recognise them, or that they will occur at an appropriate time. If students can be helped to take advantage of natural opportunities, so much the better, but we must realise that in most cases we have to create these opportunities first.

Now, to *create* realisable opportunities, we need to have a fairly clear idea of not only *what* we want the student to achieve, but why we want him to achieve it and, overall, how we would like him to achieve it. (Are there, for instance, any philosophical reasons for adopting a particular teaching or learning approach?) We need to have defined the *goals* of the learning if we are to produce purposeful assignments, and our goals can well contain not only content elements (the information or information-based content skills we want him to learn) but an indication of the general *purposes* we have in mind. Do we want the student to acquire knowledge by carrying out the assignment — to apply skills — to extend or develop his experience? Furthermore, although it may not be explicit in our goals, we need (ignoring outside constraints for the while) to decide how we would like him to carry out the assignment in general terms — by inquiry techniques — by being taught — by practising — by a combination of ways? Perhaps we can express this quite complex concept in the form of a diagrammatic table (opposite) which in itself may lead us to recognise that any learning goals involve an achievement of a number of purposes. Thus we may want a student to acquire knowledge (content) by investigating and interpreting information (development of existing learning skills).

So, to create opportunities that can be realised — to make purposeful assignments — we must be concerned first to

An activity can get the learner

to		*by*	*of*	*through*
stimulate his interest in	knowledge	inculcation	facts	assimilation (passive learning)
acquire	content skills[1]	consolidation	objects	investigation
modify	learning skills[2]	development	people	interpretation
apply	concepts	formation (formulation)	events	manipulation (practice)
pass on to others	experiences	use (manipulation)	instruction	interaction
		communication (presentation)	opinions	presentation
			attitudes	
			problems	
			ideas (theories, etc)	
			techniques	

1. Content skills are those specific skills derived from and applied to the information element of your learning (eg, maths calculations; ability to read maps . . .).
2. Learning skills are generic skills of the kind described in Chapter 3.

identify activities appropriate to a particular piece of learning, thence to design assignments (group or individual) to incorporate those activities. The final shape of an assignment may well depend on what sort of activities you want the learner to carry out in order:

(a)   to experience something and/or
(b)   to reach any goals you have set, or agreed with him, and on what other influences may affect your choice of activities.

Perhaps the first question, then, is 'How do you define an activity?'. Obvious, you may say — but is it? Which of the following, for example, would you say could be classed truly as an activity?

— To acquire knowledge
— To find out some information
— To write
— To summarise information from a book
— To write a book

You might like to look at these and decide for yourself.

We would say:

— *to acquire knowledge*
— *to find out some information* } are not activities

— *to write*
— *to summarise information from a book* } are activities

— *to write a book* is not an activity — it is a complex task involving a whole host of activities.

To take the last one first, it was not intended as a trick; all too often we produce assignments in which we identify only some of the activities necessary — a point we will pursue later.

Meanwhile, back at the ranch . . . we would probably agree that '*to acquire knowledge*' does not describe an activity but a purpose of undertaking some learning. You may well, on the other hand, have put down '*to find out*' as an activity: the phrase is after all almost indissolubly linked with the so-called 'activity method'. But is it an identifiable learning activity? Perhaps the easiest answer to the question 'is this an activity?' is to identify whether the statement gives you a good idea of HOW it (whatever 'it' is) is to happen.

Can you say roughly, or better still precisely, what the person or people carrying out the so-called activity will be doing? In this respect 'finding out . . .' is too vague; it might indicate any one of a number of specific activities. On the other hand you, like us, might have been a little unhappy about 'to write'. It is certainly an activity — you may well have just been indulging in it — but it is a very general one and with no indication of *purpose* or *level of* skill involved. We suggest that general activities, to be useful in terms of learning, need to be used mainly as qualifiers; eg, to summarise information from a book (a reasonable general activity) by *writing* it in his own words . . . or by *telling* the teacher . . . .

On the other hand 'summarising' information, or 'noting' or 'combining' or 'memorising' are all fairly specific terms which at our level can be thought of as single indentifiable learning activities. It is true that. if we go to the depths of some analyses it is possible to define, say 'summarising' (in writing) as consisting of: reading material; extracting salient points by noting them down; combining those points into a shorter description in the student's own words. If you wish to break activities down to that level or even lower there is no reason why you shouldn't, but at the level of outlining assignments you only need to do it if you need to isolate the specific skills involved. For general purposes 'summarising' is enough to describe what needs to be done and is specific enough to alert you to the need for ensuring that the student has the necessary skills, or recognising that if he hasn't there is a problem to overcome.

On page 61 is a list of the likely activities — not all at the same level — which may be useful as an aide-mémoire; the permutations are up to you, though various other factors in designing assignments may help to determine them. In particular there are two possible main reasons for designing an individual or group assignment.

(1) We may want the student to acquire, or modify, specific knowledge, content skills, etc, which we have identified beforehand — say, to learn specific items about the physical geography of the British Isles or learn how to add fractions. In this case the nature of the information may well indicate very strongly *how* we are likely to be able to frame the assignment (is it practical, like learning to manipulate decimals in which the skill may have to be taught, or factual knowledge which might be taught or found out?).

(2) We may have the development of specific learning skills predominant in our minds — eg, we may want a student to acquire knowledge by 'finding out' but we are not unduly worried about what knowledge he learns. It is the acquisition skills we want to concentrate on. They in turn will tend to determine the specific activities: we shall find useful content that will fit in with them. Naturally these elements can combine. It is probably true, however, that at individual assignment level one or other will tend to dominate, so when we get down to writing assignments we may need to specify closely what we mean in terms of activities relevant to achieving our goals.

Subject of activity act on	Activity stem by	using
data	noting	writing
objects	comparing	speaking
people	observing	listening
events	summarising	reading
situations	memorising	drawing
instructions	practising	looking
opinions	combining	thinking
attitudes	exchanging	manipulating
ideas	copying	
techniques	translating	
	calculating	
	associating	
	recalling	
	collecting	
	extracting	
	expressing	
	repeating	
	identifying	
	locating	
	constructing	
	explaining	

For example we may wish a student to acquire certain knowledge (content) and we want him, other things being equal, to do it by finding out for himself and interpreting information, and then consolidating his learning. Thus relevant activities might be

— *locating* two relevant sources of
  information
— *extracting* the information from each by   acquisition
  reading for meaning and *noting* in *writing*
— *comparing* the information to assess
  what to retain   consolidation
— *summarising* his findings in writing.

On the other hand if we want him to acquire the information by assimilating (being taught) it, perhaps because of lack of time or learning skills, we might have as relevant activities that he should *listen to* or *read* information provided by the teacher, should *note* important points and *explain* them verbally to a group. Again you may not be over-worried by content as such. You might simply want a student to develop the skill of information extraction and interpretation that he has been taught. You may therefore still want him to

— *locate* one or more sources of information
— *extract* common information from each source
— *note* the differences (compare the information)
— *summarise* his findings in writing

but the whole emphasis is different, the assignment structure being designed to reinforce the skill, not the information being sought.

The difference is that in one case the available content or information you want him to learn may determine how you go about it — if there are no suitable sources available for him to hunt up, you may *have* to provide it — while in the other case what you want practised is likely to determine exactly what he does and will influence your choice of information content — it must be at a level of difficulty he can handle with techniques he has been taught, and that in turn may restrict what to give him. Had you thought of that as a factor when choosing material for a child to 'find out' information from? In effect, what we are doing is using in each case the clarification of our goals and purposes (the reasons for attaining goals) to select from the list on page 57 specific activities that will be likely to achieve them. You, as the assignment compiler, may end up with various possible combinations of activities; which you choose is your responsibility but by choosing you will consciously or unconsciously have already made several other decisions about the characteristics of the learning you are initiating — and one of the difficulties is that we often make these decisions quite empirically. In a moment we will look more closely at what influences them but before we do you might like to try the exercise below — it will allow you, given various decisions already made for you, to evaluate how useful the checklist of activities may be to you.

Suppose you have initiated an 'idea' for learning which appears to be dependent on content (ie, it is that aspect which strikes you first as important): let us say you decide you 'want the students to consider apartheid in South Africa to give them some idea of the human problems involved' — well, that may be a socially-aware aim but it has led to many formless discussions! Clarification of your goals, however, might show that by the end of the learning, the students should be able to:

(a) state the basic principles behind the general concept of apartheid
(b) describe, without bias, how the concept is applied in practice
(c) express an opinion on the desirability or otherwise (in human terms) of the concept as practised in South Africa, supporting opinion with factual evidence.

Given these goals, you might like to work out the types of activity (by function) that would be needed to achieve them, and the *possible* specific activities that could fulfil those functions . . . within the context of an individualised approach that wants students to find out by their own effort so far as possible (ie, don't plan this as a teaching lesson: assume it is either for individuals or for a small group of your students and that for part of the time at least they will have to work without your presence since you are occupied with others).

Function	Specific activities possible
You might need activities to:	
(a) *stimulate interest*	perhaps a talk; a film; an article
(b) inculcate 'the background knowledge' and form *concepts*	*locate* information sources, *extract* information *compare* and { individually? *evaluate* { in pairs?
	write down findings in what form?
(c) form or develop opinions (note that the objectives indicate the formation of *attitude* is not a deliberate work activity	*discuss* their findings in a seminar group or (for individuals) – *discuss* in a tutorial; *write* their views backed by evidence?

Decisions, however, are rarely made entirely for you; you will in practice need to consider various factors if you are to end up with an assignment rather than just a list of *possible* activities – and it may be worth reiterating here that while you may not even consciously identify these as problems when designing a *teaching* activity, the design of learning assignments is much more dependent on identifying them in advance.

Your final choice of activities, format and desired results should therefore ideally take into account a number of factors which will vary with individual situations but which can be broadly summed up under two headings and which apply whether you are designing your own assignments or seeing if existing materials will suit your purpose. The relevant ones are discussed below.

Student factors

It is conventional at this point, especially for educational technologists, to talk blandly about 'student characteristics' in which they include individual ability, attainment, home background, colour of socks and various other useful items. Don't. At this stage we are not really concerned with individuals, odd though it may seem, but with the general student body. Unless you intend always to design separately for each individual person you must be concerned now with work that can, it is hoped, be undertaken:

(a)   by a number of students from any one group
(b)   by successive groups of students in years to come.

The factors we need to consider are simply those which you can identify as common to a group, or those implied by the goals you have worked out — presumably with your students as a whole in mind. Other more subtle ones (eg, that James X can hardly read) come into the picture when you translate your design into actual pieces of work or select appropriate assignments for individuals but at present we need to look at three things only.

(i)   What learning and content skills relevant to the desired goals can you reasonably expect the students to have and at what degree of competence? These may determine for instance, if you have to feed in information or can expect them to find it; whether you have to give them the answers to any incidental calculations or can expect them to take these in their strides.

(ii) Do you have any strong reasons for wanting the assignment to be ingoing (ie, just for the student's benefit) or outgoing (deliberately designed so that as part of it the student has to interact with others, for example to give a talk on his findings rather than writing you an essay about them)? This may well determine the whole shape of the assignment.

(iii) Are any particular people patterns desirable? Should this be a set of individual activities? Is collaboration or interaction desirable, so that part of it should be specifically designed for pair or small group work? Why, and at what points?

Now 'people patterns' are one aspect or 'dimension' of the learning scene we talked about in Chapter 1 and it is at this point that practical consideration of those other dimensions becomes important — we might call them the 'teacher factors'.

Teacher factors
(a) Control pattern: How tightly or loosely are you as the teacher/manager going to structure the actual assignment? This may well depend on the goals you and the student worked out and on what learning skills he has but within those constraints you have to make the decision. It may well determine which of a selection of activities you write in (eg, is he going to *listen* and *note* (because you have control) or *locate* information, *extract* and *assess* it . . . etc. It will certainly influence choice of the overall methods you want to employ and those in turn limit the range of activities that are relevant.

(b) Content pattern: All things being equal, do you want to:

(i)   make the assignment self-contained (ie, transferring your teaching — you as 'resource' — on to the assignment so that you provide everything the student needs)?

(ii) make it partly self-contained and partly dependent on other resources (some variety of 'resource assisted'); in which case is it going to be 'you' assisted by resources or the other way round?

(iii) base it entirely on using resource materials (ie, simply a set of guides or instructions which lead the students to carry out activities using external sources)? WHY? What good reasons can you find for taking any one of these courses of action?

It may be worthwhile expressing the process so far in diagrammatic form to summarise what we have been doing (see page 67). The addition of these factors to your goals. and possible activity patterns will almost certainly give you a very clear idea of what you can and cannot do so far as the learning requirements are concerned.

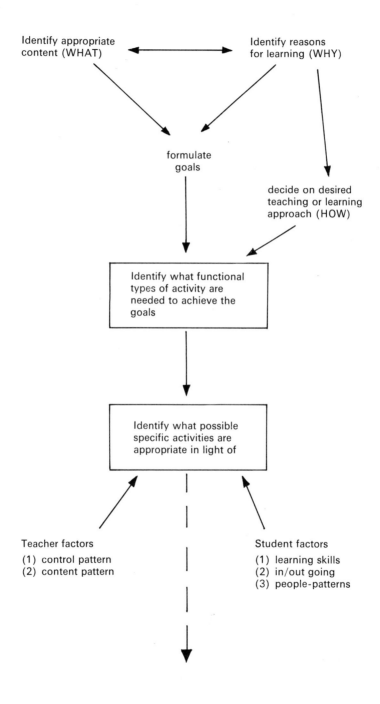

Thus to take the small 'discussion' exercise on apartheid a little further; you have a possible range of activities — whether you agreed with our assessment or included other activities of your own. Why not look to see what student and teacher factors might be relevant and how any one might influence you in picking particular activity patterns. You might find the checklist on page 73 of some help as an aide-mémoire.

If you recollect, we identified stimulating interest, inculcating knowledge and forming concepts, and forming or developing opinions as types of activity and provided several alternative ranges of activities for each. Let us for the moment leave 'stimulating interest': as an individualised activity this is much more likely to have come about through the students expressing interest. In inculcating knowledge and concepts, however, you are going to have the basic (content pattern) alternatives of:

(1)   'teaching' the information content and letting them make notes — not perhaps appropriate to an individualised activity if you can only devote part of your time to it

(2)   providing a pack of information

(3)   guiding students to study external reference sources and to compile their own background information.

In the case of either (2) or (3) you may also simply let them loose on the information or provide them with guidelines as to what to look for. Your choice of combinations is dictated by what learning skills in information processing you expect the students to have (student factor) and how closely you want to control what is done. The content pattern (1, 2 or 3) may also be influenced by what information is readily available and in what form, but that we'll discuss later.

This leaves us with what, in a controversial subject, is likely to be the most important part. Obviously group discussion springs to mind, since *interaction* would seem an important element in forming opinions. But the skills the students have, and your decision on whether it should be ingoing or outgoing, may well determine how you approach it: no doubt, if the students have discussion skills, you can simply get them all to collect the same basic information (by providing packs?) and then discuss — this may be where you take part: or you might get individuals to research different sources or aspects and then contribute information to a whole which can be discussed . . . or . . . an individual student on the other hand could achieve these goals but his pattern of activities would be more circumscribed — his interaction would have to come from writing and possibly from a tutorial.

You will have noticed, I'm sure, that any of the alternatives may also be influenced by another set of factors which in teaching one takes in one's stride — but which, in producing individualised learning, again needs careful consideration. These are what you might call *outside constraints* and can be summed up as:

— your real pupils
— the learning resources (information sources, etc) available
— the school organisation.

They include such items as the spread of ability in your student group; whether you have freedom to organise your time or whether you are constrained by the school timetable; how much information is available for the pupils to work on or how much you will have to research. (If the latter is important you may tend towards common 'packs' but are these invariably the best answer?) There is little point in discussing them in detail here since we shall meet them all later on. At this point their importance is in alerting you to ask yourself whether any of them are likely to inhibit or facilitate what you want to do.

For example, if you have decided to let students go at their own pace does the school timetable allow for different students spending varying amounts of time on the same work? Are there any overall limitations on time which might mean you would either have to limit the scope of work or, say, provide some information instead of letting individuals find it out for themselves?

If you consider your possible activities in the light of all these factors, then the outline of your assignment probably becomes much clearer. If we go back for a moment to the 'playwriting' analogy of Chapter 1, you are now at the stage where you are working out the plot — setting up the story line (the chain of activities, the people patterns); seeing what general scene settings it will need (control pattern, content pattern); deciding what characteristics the players will need to have (the student factors). Having worked these out, like any playwright you then have to translate your ideals into reality — and that means either writing the script (preparing the assignment) and then adapting it to various theatre conditions or writing the script with particular theatre conditions in mind. Both ways have their advantages and disadvantages. In the first you decide what you feel needs to be learnt and then modify to suit your students — which is what you would do, for instance, when adapting commercial materials or collaborating with other teachers. The advantage is that you have freedom to determine the ideal; the corresponding disadvantage is that you may then have to reconsider or alter quite a lot of your initial work in the light of reality (you might, so to speak, have to cut the play, make do with less than ideal scene settings because of theatre limitations, alter your cherished script because the cast you have is not the one you wanted!)

The other way is to bear your immediate circumstances in mind from the very start (eg, the known characteristics of your current student group, the space and time you have available at the moment) and deliberately design to suit those conditions. The advantages are that you are likely to end up with something that fits your present needs without having to go through the adaptation process; the corresponding disadvantage is that what you produce may be *too* specific. You may have to do it all over again next time because it does not suit another group: it is the difference, as it were, between a bespoke and an off-the-peg suit. In practice what tends to happen when producing assignments of our own is that we compromise, working out what we want but keeping present constraints in the backs of our minds in case they may dictate what we cannot do. It may be helpful to express this in diagrammatic terms to complete our picture of the process to date (see page 71).

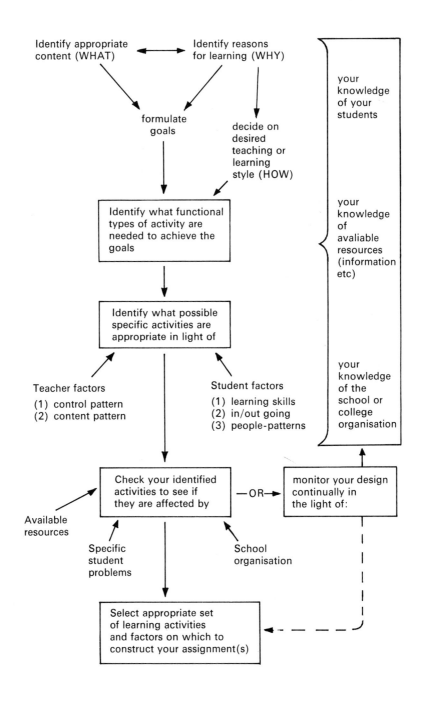

Ideally of course we all evaluate these aspects in all our planning: in practice it is all too easy to miss the one(s) that may make nonsense of all your careful work. We have therefore compiled a checklist that may prove useful — and if you feel it is all too complicated remember that any fresh collection of skills does seem so until it becomes more or less automatic. After a while the checklist becomes simply an occasional aide-mémoire just as a checklist for an aircraft pilot is: he has learnt how to fly the thing or else he wouldn't be there; what he is doing is simply checking that something vital has not been overlooked.

Alternatively you can think of your completed plan as a jigsaw where all the pieces interlock and you will not get a full picture if some are missing — indeed some people may complain that the process is far too like making a jigsaw in that it is prescriptive.

What they forget is that if you are making it you can decide the shape, size and what sort of picture you are going to draw; all the structure does is tell you if you have got your design complete.

Brief checklist for assignment planning
1. Have you identified, for any given assignment:

    — the goals
    — the approach you would like
    — any prerequisite knowledge
            content skills   ⎫ for the approach
            learning skills ⎭ you like

2. Do the students have the prerequisites?
    YES NO
        ↓
        Are you able to remedy this in advance
        OR
        Have you modified your *approach* and/or
        your *content pattern* to take account of it?

3. Have you identified activities appropriate to:

    — the goals and content?
    — the approach you are using?
    — the students' attainments and abilities?

4. Have you determined how (and if) you are to control the learning?

5. Are you clear as to whether you want the learning to be:

    — ingoing or outgoing?
    — composed of any particular people patterns?
    — carried out by any particular content pattern (self-contained; resource-based, etc)?

6. Have you determined the effects of outside constraints?

    — timetabling limitations, if any?
    — effects of any range of ability grouping?
    — availability of any resources you may need?
    — external curriculum pressures (exams, etc)?

Interlude

Up to now we have been discussing the underlying structure of 'individualising' the work of our students and hopefully conducting some sort of a dialogue, however crude. Yet even if you can identify at any time what you and the students want to do, how you want to do it and why, and what constraints there are, then you are still left with the problems of translating these skeletal ideas into reality; techniques of teaching do not automatically provide a good basic training for this. The remainder of this book is therefore devoted to a series of sections giving practical hints – some of which may be more helpful than others, depending on your circumstances. They are not intended to do your job for you but to alert you to problems which have been found to crop up again and again and to give you some indications as to how those problems might be solved. If you like to return to our play analogy, having got a plot we now have actually to write the script, bearing possible casts in mind, to divide it into actors' 'parts' and then to produce and stage manage it – always remembering that we may want to make provision for some impromptu drama. Just to add to the *angst*, the 'audience' are likely to be the students who are participating and we are undoubtedly going to have to act as our own critics!

Now, hopefully, we can agree that the major problems of *organising* individualised work of any sort are threefold:

(1) the actual planning and *organisation* of assignments, resources needed to implement them, the environment in which they will be carried out

(2) the *management* of all these things and of the learners so as to facilitate the learning taking place successfully and to the satisfaction of both you and the students

(3) the *evaluation* or examination of what is going on in order to find out if anything is wrong and to see if you can improve it in any way.

Indeed you may well want to start with the latter for there are two possible ways of approaching individualised learning.

You may be happy to do what we have been discussing in the early part of this book — what might be called a 'pre-structured' approach in which you — and your students? — have tried to work out in advance what you want to do and what the implication of various courses of action would be. On the other hand there may be times when, quite reasonably, you decide that you want to individualise work but you deliberately do *not* want to set goals, etc — you want to initiate genuinely independent learning where the students decide and control what they are doing. In that case we suggest that the need for evaluation becomes very important. You need to be able to look at what work the student has done and to answer the questions what did he achieve, was it worth the time spent, and what criteria do you use to judge it? In that case you may like to go straight to Chapter 9 and start from there. Otherwise the choice is really yours. Each of the following chapters takes one aspect of the individualising process within the whole situation and as page 76 shows the process tends to be cyclic rather than linear . . . you can organise resources to give you information on which to write assignments . . . or design assignments and then sort out the resources to match them . . . or . . . Thus the following chapters are not sequential but a number of discrete sections with objectives for each to tell you what we hope each will achieve and with assumptions clearly stated at the beginning. They will also try to give you experience of various types of information displays and learning tools.

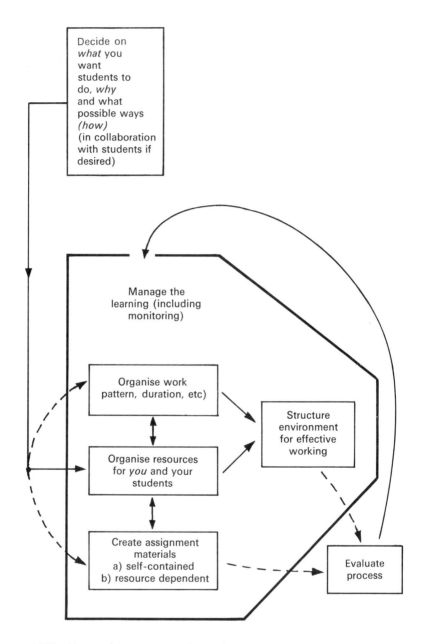

Decide on *what* you want students to do, *why* and what possible ways *(how)* (in collaboration with students if desired)

Manage the learning (including monitoring)

Organise work pattern, duration, etc)

Organise resources for *you* and your students

Create assignment materials
a) self-contained
b) resource dependent

Structure environment for effective working

Evaluate process

NOTE: If you wish to go towards true independent learning, remember that THE STUDENT MUST BE CAPABLE OF DOING ALL OR MOST OF THESE OPERATIONS HIMSELF.

6. Organising patterns of work

Goals

This section is intended to help you identify and use some organisational resources to facilitate achievement of learning goals. By the end of it you should be able to:

(a) identify various patterns of work organisation particular to individualised learning or teaching (eg, project) and their characteristics; state some advantages and limitations of each approach

(b) identify five possible ways of keeping track of student progress (monitoring) and state the limitations and implications for their design and use

(c) identify problems in controlling the learning activities of individuals and suggest outline solutions to them.

You will *not,* from reading this, be better equipped to design and administer tests and other assessment devices, but the information index (p195) gives details of books which go into detail on these matters. In addition, if you work through Appendix 3 you should be able with some practice, using verbal or diagrammatic means, to:

(i) define the boundaries and content of a topic area (information content) or of a skills area (content skills)

(ii) identify for any given content area, elements of work suitable for development of learning skills; content skills; knowledge/concepts.

Content

The chapter is in three sections:

— patterns of work organisation (p 77)
— monitoring student progress (p 91)
— controlling the learning situation (p 94)

1. Patterns of work organisation

One of the first tenets of 'resource-oriented' work is that 'resources' do not simply imply physical things: they can also be ways of organising the work both at 'lesson' level and in the broader context of classroom organisation. This chapter discusses some of the problems peculiar to organising individualised as opposed to class-group work.

There are several methods of organising such work but all have some problem in common. You will always need to:

(1)   identify whether, for the student, the work is to be basically closed-ended (ie, will lead him to predetermined goals) or open-ended (ie, designed to lead on to one or more other areas of work). If it is to be open-ended just *how* open-ended will it be?

(2)   identify where the student and yourself will need feedback — information and assistance — on how he is progressing.

(3)   decide how to build in checks on achievement if they are needed. What sort of checks do you need? Are they to be formal or informal?

(4)   choose which available resource materials, if any, that you want to incorporate in the work.

(5)   ensure a variety of work for the student.

Now you are likely to have identified general goals for your students and sorted out the kinds of activities you want the students to undertake before you start considering the work in detail. You are likely, too, to be thinking in terms of single assignments at this stage because we tend to plan in detail a 'lesson' at a time. Yet teaching is organised not just by lessons but by courses and schemes of work, so what are *their* individualised work equivalents? You might like to pause and jot some down before continuing.

Did you have any of the following?
— Individual or group assignments
— Projects
— Structured work schemes
— Student work contracts
— Independent learning schemes

All are methods of organising individuals, or groups of students for active learning. You may or may not have included 'contracts' although they have been around in various guises for some time; remember the Dalton Plan?

On the other hand you may well have put down 'topics' or 'topic work' which was omitted deliberately. Surely a *topic* is not a method of organising work? True, 'topic work' is often equated with 'projects' but if we are exact it is nothing of the sort; it is a description of subject matter content. A project may be concerned with exploring one or more *topics* but the topic itself is simply a theme on which to hang the organisation of work over a period of time; it does not imply any particular pattern of work within that theme. Thus to say you are going to 'do topic work' simply indicates that you have decided that information content is an important element. You could cover the topic by class teaching, by one or more projects, by sets of individual assignments.

Given that, you might like to pause for a moment and try to define in your own terms what constitutes the patterns of organisation we have labelled 'assignments', 'structured schemes', 'work contracts', 'projects'.

Perhaps the easiest way of illustrating the concepts involved is to put down an example. Thus, in geography, let's say...

(1) The goal of an *assignment* for a student might be 'to be able, when he has finished, to read a simple contour map so as to identify from it salient physical features of a landscape' (note that this is a content skill which may need teaching).

(2) A *project* in the same 'topic area' might be a land-use study of the area around the school or college in order that the students may
(a) become familiar with their environment and be able to describe the way in which the land is used and how those uses have developed (information/concept content)
(b) develop specific skills (which you must identify) in interviewing; mapping and recording; extracting and synthesising information; reporting findings as an inter-active group (learning skills).

Such a project might well include (1) as one of a number of pre-organised assignments which would provide a basis for the project while leaving room for individual development of work.

(3)   A *structured scheme* in this area might consist of a number of graduated assignments designed to teach students various skills of reading and making maps — so that it in turn might stand on its own or form part of the 'resource bank' for a *project* like that mentioned above.

(4)   A work *contract* in the same area might simply consist of you agreeing with the student that as part of his geography syllabus he would be proficient in reading and interpreting maps (and in various other skills or knowledge) by the end of a given period of time — say half a term. You might 'build in' a number of assignments which he has to complete as evidence of progress or you might leave the detailed organisation of the work entirely to him and just suggest items which may help him. But remember: 'GO AND FIND OUT' is NOT A VIABLE OPTION unless you are certain he has the necessary learning skills and that the relevant information is available at the time it is wanted.

That having been said, it may be worth looking more closely at the organisational problems of the various forms of learning activity: the problems of providing actual student materials we will leave to Chapter 8.

Student assignments
These tend to form the basis of individualised work because they are usable both by themselves and as part of almost any more complex *organised* scheme. An assignment is basically a translation into terms understood by the student of the 'plot' created by formulating goals; selecting appropriate activities according to the way in which you want the learning to take place; examining them in the light of outside constraints. In theory, if all these factors allow, an assignment could simply be a verbal or written instruction to 'go and do so and so, and

bring it to your teacher when you have finished'. In practice it is likely to contain more if only because an individualised assignment should be capable, all other constraints being satisfied, of standing on its own; like the proverbial essay it should at least have a beginning, a middle and an end! You might like to jot down the basic elements which you would need to include.

What about a title or label for a start. Did you include that? It really is needed if only to let you both pick out the particular assignment you want to work on. Then you might need the following.

1. A brief introduction as to what the assignment is about. How far are you going to go? Just 'This will help you to do xx . . . ', or are you going to give him a stated goal to aim at?
2. A clear indication of any information resources you want him to use. In how much detail do you refer to them?
3. Any leading questions you may want to ask in order to direct his attention to specific points (how you phrase these may depend on what learning skills he has).
4. An indication of when (if at all) you want him to contact you — to check progress or at points of difficulty?
5. A description of what results you expect him to provide and how he should present them (to you? to others? in writing? by talking?).
6. Possibly, an indication of how long the assignment might take.

Now whether you put down all or any of these, we cannot tell. You may well have gone off on another track entirely and be cursing the writer for being obscure and keeping on asking questions that are almost impossible to answer! If so, sorry, but one of the principles of individualising learning is that the learner (which in this case is you as the reader) does something rather than just accepting passively what is put before him. Another principle is that when he does something (ie, performs a learning activity) he gets feedback on the results of his actions. If you sometimes feel frustrated because we don't agree, it might be worth remembering that your students can easily feel the same if you get your assignments wrong. The broader and more open ended questions are, the more awkward it is to frame acceptable answers, and therefore the more need there is for immediate feedback and for explanation of the results.

Indeed a skeleton assignment of any kind is the one that can most easily produce misunderstanding and frustration. It can only be used with certainty if your students have the necessary skills to carry out its instructions or suggestions. If they have not, your assignment will need to be more elaborate because it must either:

(a)   guide by getting the student to ask and answer the 'right questions at the right time' eg, 'Look at p xx. What do you notice about the . . . ', in which case *you* need to identify and examine the necessary resource items closely enough to know what the student is likely to find
       and/or

(b)   teach by giving the student information and, if needs be, guiding his interaction with it (eg, if he has difficulty in locating relevant information you may incorporate it in the assignment as an information sheet) or, more specifically, you may give him 'learning material' with which he interacts. Thus, in our geographical example, you might either give him facts about contours and get him to extract and apply them, or you might give him what amounts to instruction in which the relevant points are brought out and he is asked to make specific responses — as you have been asked to do at various points in this book.

In either case your assignment tends then to become more and more *self-contained* and to depend less and less on outside resources.

We might then be able to summarise the main types of assignment. Again you might like to do this, before going on.

The main forms may be summarised as follows.

(1)   *Basically   instructions   or   suggestions   only.*   The

advantages are that the assignments take less time to prepare and are more 'independent' in their operation. The corresponding disadvantages are that if the student does not already have the learning skills implied by the instructions, he may not learn — may indeed waste his time — and if you do not *know* what resources are available the same thing may happen.

(2) *Instructions/suggestions plus guidance* on how to carry them out, either by questions relating to 'outside' materials and/or by incorporating information. The student can be enabled to judge progress by periodical feedback. An advantage is that you can overcome difficulties for the student: a disadvantage is that writers tend to get in a rut.

(3) *Teaching indirectly* by making the student interact with structured information. This means that you have control over the learning but it is not an easy thing to do.

Note that in both (2) and (3), information may be provided in one of two guises — as a stimulus and basis for work but requiring access to outside resources as well, either to complete or to extend it; or as the sole basis on which work is to be done, without recourse to outside materials.

So much for the organisational problems of producing assignments but assignments are not the be-all and end-all of individualised work — though they are often thought to be when people interpret it as individual instruction. Many pieces of work that are identified as separate assignments are not really that at all; they are integral parts of a scheme of structured learning and do not stand on their own.

Structured learning schemes

Anybody involved in individualising work will have met with — and perhaps tried to construct — one of these for there is a large amount of material available commercially, especially in literacy work. Their characteristics are:

(1) they usually consist of linked pieces of work, of assignment pattern but designed so that the student

progresses through a sequence of them building up skills or knowledge

(2) they are usually intended to achieve a series of specific goals and are normally concerned mainly with development of content skills (eg, reading) or learning skills (eg, communicating ideas)

(3) the individual materials in them are often of a similar, repetitive pattern because they are designed constantly to reinforce student performance in those skills; a familiar format is often a help

(4) there is usually a strong didactic element: the individual 'assignments' teach or reinforce directly.

What is less often identified is that much teacher-produced 'individualised work material', rather than being genuinely enquiry-based or composed of separate assignments, has many of the characteristics of structured work schemes. So long as it is inculcating skills it thus has similar advantages and disadvantages, but in many cases the concept has been modified to relate to information content. Many of the innovative humanities 'projects' of secondary schools fall into this category and there the characteristics of structure that are adapted to skills work can become massive disadvantages – the progression from one to another 'sheet' loses much of its point if the student simply accumulates information instead of reinforcing and extending skill; the similarity of format, worksheet after worksheet, becomes boring rather than supportive. This is not to say content-based schemes are inevitably bad, only to point out that their production and use need especially careful consideration.

The organisational problems of structured 'schemes' are thus twofold:

(1) the problems of effective use of existing schemes

(2) the problems of producing home-made materials – which will be discussed in Chapter 8.

The problems of organising the *use* of a structured scheme are inherent in its structure.

1. It is likely because of its complexity to be expensive and

this means that it may be used almost to the exclusion of other materials on the same subject or skills area. This attitude is likely to be reinforced by the scheme's originators who often see it as doing the whole job, but you should be warned against it. Using any skills-based scheme too slavishly instead of intermittently can well lead to:
— student boredom
— omission of some aspects of the learning (most skills-based schemes only cover certain aspects of their 'subject')
— lack of relevance to other learning being undertaken by the student.
2. It may give the teacher a false feeling of being in control because of its careful structuring. Yet if he does not watch out, those very characteristics can become disadvantages. A structured scheme to be successful may not need to be worked right through — many include diagnostic elements so that a student covers only those assignments he needs. On the other hand students do need to complete individual pieces of work and if timetabling, etc, is such that some students rarely or never complete the work they start then the scheme may be a failure for them.
3. You need to avoid being 'run' by the material. Are you aware of what it claims to do and what it misses out? Do you know what other resources are available which might provide extension work or a different approach for students who are not progressing? Do the goals and other factors you have analysed indicate that the scheme has a definite major role or do you want to use it simply as an ancillary? If so, where does it fit in?

Structured schemes have their place in any learning scheme just as freedom of student choice does but neither should be the major part unless all prerequisites indicate it is possible. More useful, though more difficult to organise properly, is the range of compromises between rigid structure and student freedom (the two main examples of which are 'contract' and 'project' work). Both are frequently used as soon as a teacher moves from a formal teaching situation: both often fall down in practice because of lack of planning and non-availability of student assignments when needed.

'Contract work'

In essence contracts are a means of assigning more responsibility to individual students or small groups by agreeing with them that they should try to achieve certain goals or cover certain areas of work in a specified period of time. The essential element is *agreement* which means that you as the teacher must have worked out what is involved, be fairly certain that it is attainable and that the student is clear about what he has to achieve.

The *crunch,* on which many assignment or contract plans have fallen down in the past is that the contract must be capable of achievement by the students. This means that you as the teacher/manager must have investigated the subject matter area concerned, identified the relevant resources, the possible areas of difficulty, the various constraints (time, etc) so that:

(a)   you can agree 'content' that is realistic for individuals (covers vital elements and is within their capabilities)

(b)   you can devise assignments to help students where needed

(c)   you can provide ways of monitoring students' progress and diagnosing problems so that you can help them actively when required.

It also means that, unless you adopt some variant of the 'resource heap' approach now fashionable in higher education you have to be prepared to organise and produce a lot of varied assignments together with some form of mechanism for monitoring or controlling the learning — and this is the Achilles heel of so many contract schemes: it just does not get done. The 'resource heap' approach tries to avoid this by simply providing a mass of relevant or hopefully relevant material and then putting the responsibility on the student to find what he wants and use/interpret it. It has many features in common with extreme free-discovery techniques and like them it is the nearest thing, it is claimed, to true independent learning.

It may work in higher education, though one has the suspicion that it may often be adopted more to ease the burden on the lecturer rather than to facilitate learning, but in the earlier years of secondary schooling its adoption on such a scale is dubious – it assumes your student already has a wide range of information-handling skills and furthermore is mature enough to discriminate between 'relevant' and 'irrelevant' material. If he cannot do that and if you are not sure that the 'heap' contains all or most of the information he will need, then we suggest you are really just abrogating your responsibility as a teacher.

A *contract* approach then requires a careful analysis of the learning to be undertaken (remember our learning-country analogy in Chapter 3) and a willingness to use that to build up a series of possible assignments which one can eventually assemble to form a basis. Its main advantage is that it is inherently flexible and can be built up gradually; it does not *have* to be produced all in one piece. Apart from this it has many characteristics in common with the other major compromise, the *project* approach, and many of the skills involved in project design are also applicable to *contract* planning and implementation. The major difference is that in one case you are planning a number or series of related assignments for individuals; in the other you are organising an area of work to which a number of students may contribute . . . the dividing line is not always precise!

Projects

The 'project approach', or in more limited form, the occasional 'project' lasting from a few weeks to a term or more, has always been considered as one of the mainstays of individualised work; it has been seen as equally applicable to primary, middle and secondary school work and has even crept into further education.

Yet what is it, and, more important, are there any useful ways in which one can make more effective use of the approach?

All too often, we suggest, a project is simply thought of as a way of occupying a period of time without clear goals in mind. It is assumed, especially in primary or lower secondary situations, that if you turn a group of students loose on a bank of related resources and provide some additional stimuli (eg, visits), learning and pupil motivation will inevitably result. Too often, indeed, the *topic* — the subject area in which the children are to work — is identified as being synonymous with *project* and little help is given on why that topic has been chosen or on how to approach it. Yet a project — if we take it as a purposeful investigation of a stated area of work — can be used for many purposes, and since it invariably occupies a considerable block of time, it should be exploited to the full.

So what is a 'project'? Wouldn't you agree that in a scheme of individualised work it should deliberately be not just an investigation of some knowledge/conceptual area for the sake of content, but also a vehicle for developing various learning and/or content skills in the students? If you accept that, we can define a *project* as a way·of organising work, either for individuals or individuals-in-a-group which:

(a)   provides a framework — in the sense of a defined area of study
(b)   encourages and guides the students to investigate that area in an organised fashion to achieve certain goals by using resources other than just the teacher
(c)   allows for students developing their own interests within the overall framework and even, if it is felt desirable, extending their work outside the original project area
(d)   allows for individual study over a period of time extending from a few days to a term or more
(e)   in group projects provides for pulling together the results of investigations to provide a communal result, perhaps as an exhibition.

This, you may say, is self-evident — but is it? 'Dissertations' or 'special studies' that end up as rag-bags of fact because no thought was given to helping students organise them — or to ensuring they had the necessary skills beforehand; students with 'gaps' in their repertoire of skills because their lack was not identified or remedied; confused ideas about how to investigate a subject . . . all these and other problems owe something to the dangers inherent in the project approach.

At the least we suggest that you should be able to answer the following questions if you intend to take project work seriously.

(a) Can you define the topic area to be covered in sufficient detail to be able to:

   (i) identify relevant resources
   (ii) identify areas likely to be useful for particular learning purposes (development of content skills, etc).

(b) Is the project going to be based on information available:

   (i) wholly within the school/college?
   (ii) largely within the school/college?
   (iii) largely outside the school/college — and if so where? What are the problems of access?

(c) Is it to be:

   (i) a group project in which individuals may work on different aspects of a subject or topic but in which they combine at the end to contribute to a common result? (Link to (d) below.)
   (ii) a project for individuals/pairs, each of whom will complete their own study of a particular topic?

(d) Is the main object basically:

   (i) content acquisition?
   (ii) development of skills? (content? learning?)

(e) Can you see clearly how you are going to guide the students:

   (i) by the content framework only?
   (ii) by 'key' assignments plus freedom of choice?
   (iii) by a worked-out scheme of assignments?
   (iv) by guidance on how to tackle various aspects?

Your answers to (a) and (e) in particular have marked implications for the *usefulness* of the project (which is not necessarily to be equated with the success in terms of elaborateness of results).

You should also be in a position, for any particular *activity* you feel is desirable, to say: WHY it is included, WHAT you expect it to contribute to the learning, HOW you expect that contribution to be achieved. Just as clearly this book cannot answer those questions for you. It can only raise them and, perhaps, give you tools which will help you answer them.

Independent learning systems
So much for projects: there remains one 'pattern of work' which was mentioned at the beginning of this chapter and then conveniently forgotten − independent learning. Now true independent learning is by definition almost impossible to organise since only the learner can decide what is going to happen. In practice most so-called 'independent learning systems' are variants on the 'contract' pattern of work in that general goals are agreed with the learner and a certain amount of help and guidance is provided. In some cases they are even fairly tightly structured and may more fairly be called independent study − the independence lying in the absence of continuous teacher contact, and in the student's ability to vary the pace of his learning, the times at which he works and the order (other constraints permitting) in which he carries out the detailed assignments. In those respects the work organisation is subject to the same problems as other structured schemes and the only thing left to ask you to do is to pause when or if you introduce 'independent study' and examine exactly what it involves.

It may be worth noting here that so far we have been talking about *individual* individualised learning in the sense that your plans have been concerned with assignments, patterns of work and organisation that envisage a collection of students as a number of independent bodies rather than as an interacting whole. True we have mentioned group assignments but the closest we have got to interaction is a project-type approach in which each student or small group does one or more learning tasks and then helps to put them all together to achieve a communal result. We have ignored the teaching situation where the group is in fact teaching itself and is covertly or overtly assessing its own progress. Yet almost every large scale project on individualisation over the last few years has come up with a need at some point for formalised group work – though more to serve psychological or social needs, it would appear, than to meet specific learning needs.

This work can of course be formal teaching as a group activity and that is not within the scope of this book. You will undoubtedly provide teaching where needed to stimulate interest, to 'tie up loose ends' or solve a common problem, to provide a forum for discussion. The psychological requirement for such activities is greatly reduced if the individualised work is organised so that students are not often left in uncertainty, so that their confidence in what they are doing is strengthened. We would, however, suggest that there is at times a learning need for interactive group assignments and that this should be identified at the stage of defining learning goals and purposes. Such group work may or may not need the presence and guidance of a teacher. In particular, interactive group assignments can be used in controversial subjects, for example to:

– provide pre-reading and initial discussion
– provide guidelines which a group may use to consider the subject together with the object of providing a balanced report
– provide an actual framework for discussion in which the group is led by the assignment material to consider aspects of a subject and to study the implications of any judgements they may make.

Monitoring individualised work

The second and by no means the least important part of organising individualised or resource-oriented work is to provide a structure and instruments whereby you can assess how well your students are doing – and one if possible whereby they can assess their own progress as well. Thus you can guide pupils who are wandering, ensure that learning problems are identified in time, record the acquisition or non-acquisition of specific skills and knowledge which you may feel are essential. Clearly the more genuinely *independent* the student learning is, the more difficult it is to monitor what is happening to everyone of a 'group' of twenty or thirty individuals. Conversely the more control you have over the learning the easier it is to identify what each student is doing and therefore to keep an eye on how he is progressing.

In practice, for individualised or resource-intensive elements of the work you have five main ways of checking what is happening. You might like to pause and note down what you think they are?

You might:

(a) *build checks into learning assignments themselves* so that students may, providing they are motivated, come to you at points which you have identified as needing your help:
   'Now go and see your teacher . . . '
   'When you have finished take this to . . . '
   'If you get the last three questions wrong . . . '

(b) *provide small tests of various kinds* to check achievement of specific assignments – ranging from spot checks, through a range of questions to practical work which demonstrates how well the learning has been assimilated

(c) *conduct informal impromptu checks* while students are working, and note the results . . . but you need to do this on a fairly systematic basis for it to be effective. Casual chat may well pick up the odd problem but you can as easily miss many more.

(d) *get a student to record for himself* what he is doing and how effectively he does it – or thinks he does it. This may well be the major way of monitoring at the 'independent learning' end of the scale.

(e) *use the actual results of the students' work* to help you judge achievement. This is a common method where work involves compilation of information or collaboration (eg, topic work in a project). Its problems are in judging *individuals'* progress especially in the development of specific learning or content skills.

In a typical learning situation, the structure of monitoring you build may well involve more than one of these methods and their eventual success will depend to some extent on the instruments you provide for recording and indicating progress. Those are likely to be various forms of tests themselves (which may form a record) and the relevant teacher and student record documents. Pages 94, 95 show briefly what is likely to be involved. Frustratingly, this is one of the areas where it is comparatively easy to give generalised advice but where anything further really needs a book in itself. The problem of *testing* — whether by formal, objective tests, essays, pieces of course work or other assessment devices — is not peculiar to individualised work and we do not propose to offer further advice on it. If you need to go into the area of test construction (eg, for CSE) you will need more specialised knowledge and we suggest that, as a start, you consult the books listed in the information index (p195) under TESTING.

Student and teacher record documents need a little more comment perhaps since, the more individualised work becomes, the more important it is to record it. In teaching one can often just keep a mark-book recording different students' progress on group assignments — all doing the same thing. In a project, however, students may be carrying out different work but you still want to note if and when each one acquires, for example, a specific content skill you have identified. Your record may therefore have to be rather different and include spaces for:

— items you want the student to complete
— skills, etc, you want the student to acquire — with indication of level of competence
— date entry made (to see, for example, if you need to test for retention)
— comments to remind you of any problems, etc.

After all, if you have a number of students following varying paths, then it becomes difficult to remember exact details of each one and it is very easy to overlook failure to achieve something — or even for you to fail to give him work designed to help him achieve that thing. There is no useful 'standard' form but in general it is probably easier to keep a record for each student (perhaps as a file) than to keep a record for each piece of *work*. It is not as easy to correlate individual work items with the achievement patterns of a whole group of students. Student record documents, on the other hand are found mainly in individualised or resource-intensive work and are important because:

(a) they give the student a record of what he has done, and if properly designed, can be a motivating factor in that he can see his progress as it is recorded

(b) they give you (or your colleagues, if the student is involved in a team-teaching situation) a quick check on how he is getting on — how much of a contracted set of tasks he has done, how much skill, etc, he has acquired.

It is conventional to visualise such documents as cards containing specific items in verbal form but they can vary widely according to the reasons for their existence. Page 95 gives three examples of student documents for different jobs and they are only examples, though it should be noted that they all include:

(i)   personal details to identify the 'owner'
(ii) some means of recording progress
(iii) an automatic record of work done (ie, completed, not necessarily with complete 'success').

If you wish to go further into the subject, you will find references in the information index (p195) under MONITORING.

Controlling the learning situation

You can have worked out all your goals, decided how to achieve them, even produced means of achieving them and ways of monitoring what is happening. All this may go for nothing unless you can also identify that there are organisational problems in actually ensuring that learning can proceed smoothly for the students.

These problems are rooted in three areas.

1. A record card for noting work done by an individual in a resource centre or similar place

NAME:		CLASS	
DATE	WORK DONE		NEXT VISIT

column for recording results, etc

Aid to staff in booking

2. A document for recording completion of a matrix of set tasks which can be worked through in any order

NAME........................		CLASS...............
SUBJECT		
TASK 1	TASK 2	TASK 3
TASK X *JF good*	TASK Y	

Teacher's initials and grade or comment when student presents results of his work or takes test

Short description of activities (either a standard 'set', with those not needed crossed through or compiled specially for individual

3. A folder for recording progress through a structured scheme

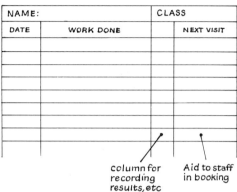

personal details

Register notes progress through the scheme

Graph plots increasing achievement (formally assessed)

1. *The physical conditions*
   - timetabling
   - arrangement of the work environment
2. *The outside contraints*
   - pressures of examinations
   - pressures of internal syllabi
   - school staff structure
3. *The nature of individual work*; in particular:
   - the problem people have in organising themselves
   - the tendency for time-wasting either deliberate or inevitable
   - the problem of supervision

Physical conditions and outside contraints are always with us; they are important mainly in their interaction with the problems inherent in the nature of individualised work and these are:

(a) the problems people have in organising themselves. To start with, we all work naturally at varying paces, and this is complicated by the fact that very few students appear able to organise their work without help. The consequence is that, unless some pressure is applied and guidance given, individualised work always takes far longer than the equivalent amount of teaching – an obscure variation, no doubt, of Murphy's Law.

(b) the tendency to increase the time spent in individual work because of problems inherent in resource-oriented study; the relevant law says 'What you want in any given situation IS ALWAYS SOMEWHERE ELSE' – and usually at the far end of the school. Thus a good deal of time is spent simply in moving about, acquiring or returning things, and this again can be increased because lack of personal motivation or organisation can lead a student to 'potter'. Some classroom studies have indicated that in extreme cases only about 10% of some students' time is actually used for purposeful work.

(c) the problem of supervision – of ensuring as far as possible that students are not just wasting time, or having to wait for attention.

Fortunately these characteristics in turn suggest at least their own outline solutions, the most important of which are:

(i) Try to ensure that the work environment is right for the particular work pattern. In particular try to cut down possible distractions by arrangement of furniture and provision of commonly needed equipment such as pencils, etc. Try, too, to reduce to the minimum the amount of movement over long distances: have the resources items you need in the classroom if possible or try to design assignments so that if a student has to go to and from somewhere, one item will occupy him for some time.

(ii) Be willing, if necessary, to apply judicious 'pressure' to limit the time taken in working out particular assignments. If you can get the students into accepting time goals for completing particular pieces of work you are half-way to beating the problem of pacing and unnecessary time-wasting.

(iii) Try to ensure that the detailed design of work fits in with any constraints you cannot alter. In particular assignments and learning materials need so far as possible to be designed so that they can be completed within any time constraints imposed by the timetable — or, if they cannot be so completed, you should try to build in 'natural breaks'. You would expect your students to be given an identifiable 'piece of work' in a teaching lesson so why should they not have the same courtesy in individualised work? With few exceptions it is not good to leave students 'hanging in the air' half-way through an assignment. If they are really interested they get frustrated; if they are indifferently motivated they may not learn effectively and the work just becomes a chore.

These comments may be general but if you have utilised the planning ideas suggested in Chapters 1–5, then the detailed solutions for any particular situation should emerge naturally. In individual work, the teacher has to become a manager and the success of the work will depend largely on the quality of his management. Management in turn can only function properly with a full knowledge of the exact situation being managed.

MONITORING

METHODS	mainly useful for
built-in checks	individual assignments
tests and other formal assessment devices	individual assignments; structured schemes; contracts
impromptu checks	project work; independent work
student judgement	projects; independent work; contracts
use of results of work	all

to be effective need	
INSTRUMENTS	IMPLICATIONS
structured assignments; teacher record (to note progress)	Assignment materials must have been carefully worked out and the appropriate feedback points/problem areas identified.
the tests; student and teacher record	Need to identify where formal tests would be appropriate and then to design them to meet particular circumstances.
teacher record to note any comments	Need to be familiar with what the student is doing — and with any skills, etc, identified as needing to be developed.
needs a student record card of some kind	May be very subjective and indicates only what the student chooses.
completed work; teacher record to note elements identified as important	Can only be done when *either* all the work is by an individual *or* when an individual's contribution can be isolated *or* where collaboration is an identified requirement.

7. Organising physical resources

Goals

This chapter is intended to help you organise the physical resources you need for your work (ie, at classroom level). By the end of it you should be able to:

(a)   identify the characteristics of any resource item in terms of its nature and its usefulness for particular tasks
(b)   identify and describe the major problems of resource organisation from the classroom teacher's point of view
(c)   index 'your' resources to retrieve (i) any given item (ii) information about items
(d)   identify appropriate methods of storing various items
(e)   provide a method of organising 'your' collection for easy retrieval and return of resource items
(f)   state the major reasons for displaying information and list some ways of doing it and their problems.

You will *not* be in a position to organise resources at school or college level.

The chapter is in five sections:

At the end is a set of guideline procedures.
If you want to go further into the matter study the information index at the back of the book.

Defining physical resources

'Organising resources' has been cited several times in this book as a very desirable concomitant of any individualised approach but the only definition offered to you so far is that 'a resource is anything that can be identified as able to contribute to the learning process at a given time'.

You may well feel justified in asking what exactly are the physical as opposed to organisational items that may meet this definition, and how you know in any particular situation whether an item really is a resource for your student or not? The answer is not easy but we can probably divide the physical items we are likely to use into three broad categories – *raw material*, which is self-explanatory; *tools*, a definition which may cover more than you think; *information-carrying* resources which include such things as books, tapes (but not tape-recorders which are tools), people or their memories, etc.

Raw material and tools have a lot in common in that they are essentially items intended to facilitate *doing* something but are not learnable from in themselves – it is *how* they are used that determines if they help indirectly in learning. An information-carrying item, however, is potentially directly valuable to anyone for learning purposes providing he or she can extract and handle the information it contains: individualised work is to a large extent about how this can be facilitated for the student.

There are minor confusions between tools and information-carrying items; you quite often hear someone saying, 'Oh, I'm teaching it by the overhead projector' or 'He's learning by the tape-recorder' – implying that it is the machine that is doing the work, whereas it is only acting as a (hopefully) appropriate medium for conveying learning information – and it is the quality of the *material* that will determine if learning takes place. So you might say that in terms of their *power* to facilitate learning, raw materials and tools are only latent – they need someone to use them, to link them with information to be of value. Information-carrying resources are more powerful. Essentially, most of them might be called *passive* in that they do not help a student to use the information they contain – which is why we are so concerned with the development of learning skills and the possible need to modify items to make them more *active* in facilitating interaction with the student and thus help his learning.

In practice, if we can once sort out exactly what we are

talking about, the organisation of raw material and tools is not a big problem so far as individualised work *per se* is concerned. Most schools have established procedures which work quite well for any learning/teaching situation. What worries most people is the problem of organising the physical items that contain *information* (books, pictures, tapes, etc) and this is clearly your problem since, to make individualised work consistently successful, you need

(1) to know as exactly as possible what information (knowledge, facts, opinions, help with content skills work) is available for you and your student to use
(2) to be able to judge the suitability of any particular piece of information-carrying material for particular individuals
(3) to be able to get hold of the item containing that information when you or the students need it.

Otherwise how can you produce assignments which may involve reference to or modification of the material?

Now unless your school or college has been utterly ruthless about centralising everything you are likely to have a number of sources of information available:

(a) books and other items held in the school library or resource centre or obtainable through it
(b) items in the local environment, where appropriate, (eg, a nature trail)
(c) your 'own' local classroom or departmental collections which pertain to your subject interest.

How do you deal with them? You could leave it all to someone else – for example a specialist librarian or organiser – which is what most of the books tell you to do. The trouble is that, once you genuinely individualise work, you are likely to find that this is not sufficient; it rarely entirely meets requirements 1 and 2 above and usually means that any 'personal' or 'departmental' collections remain squirrel hoards – and you know what the squirrel did with the nuts.

The alternative is to accept gratefully any 'outside' facilities that are available but not to *rely* on them to meet your learning needs. We are fully aware that the time of individual teachers is limited but if you agree that individualised learning situations cannot be run on the teacher's knowledge alone (ie, not 'teacher-as-resource') then some form of immediate help is needed both for you initially and *for any new colleagues or successors who may become involved in an individualised work situation you have started.*

Do notice that in all this there are really *two* operations.

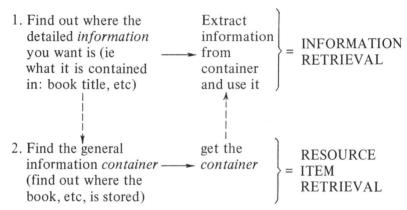

1. Find out where the detailed *information* you want is (ie ⟶ what it is contained in: book title, etc)   Extract information from container and use it   } = INFORMATION RETRIEVAL

2. Find the general information *container* ⟶ (find out where the book, etc, is stored)   get the *container*   } = RESOURCE ITEM RETRIEVAL

Please don't confuse them. All too often 'resource-based' work organisation concerns itself only with the second operation and ignores the first or assumes that it will happen automatically if a student carries out the second. It won't, which is one of the reasons much resource-oriented work is so disappointing for all concerned. So whatever the general organisation of resources in the school, we are going to suggest that the important thing for *you* initially is to have a system of your own that:

(a)   once set up, takes as little time as possible to organise and keep up to date − it may be necessary but it is an additional chore

(b)   will enable *you* (and if you want, your students) to find out quickly what information is available on any aspect of the area of knowledge you are interested in and how useful it is − irrespective of where it is located physically

(c)   will enable you to get hold of the item(s) containing specified information

(i) by efficient storage and means of retrieving items in 'your' possession — normally kept locally in your classroom, departmental stockroom, year base, etc.
(ii) by telling you where any other item can be found (eg, a particular place in the school library, a feature such as a pond in the local environment).

Any resource organisation system — and there are many — to meet these requirements must have four elements.

1. Details of what information is available and where it may be found   (INDEX)

2. Means of storing *items* so that they are properly protected and can be got at.   (STORAGE)

3. Means of locating *items* once you have decided you want the information in them and of returning them to the same place.   (RETRIEVAL)

4. Some means of stock checking so that you can be certain if the information is still available at any time.   (STOCK CONTROL)

The following pages describe suggested methods to enable you *as a classroom teacher* to achieve these aims in the context of your own local (classroom or departmental collection) situation and with the idea of using individualised work in mind. They are *not* the only methods of doing the job but have been designed specifically for this purpose. References to other general methods will be found in Appendix 1 which also displays an example of an information index.

   It may be worth pointing out that elements 2 and 4 above only become important if your local collection of materials is likely to become big. The most important part of your system is likely to be the *index* and that is what helps you do the first part of INFORMATION RETRIEVAL.

Indexing — general introduction

Indexing in independent learning terms means making available lists and descriptions of *information* which you or your students may need in the course of assignments and which should enable its user to:

1. find out what is available on $\begin{cases} \text{broad subject topics} \\ \text{(eg 'ships')} \\ \text{specific topics (eg sailing} \\ \text{clippers)} \end{cases}$

2. find out *at the same place* (ie without going to search for each item) basic information about each resource item, viz:

- contents
- level of difficulty (who is it suitable for?)
- level of interest (is it too childish for X?)
- format (does it need special equipment for use?)

Ideally it should also include some indication as to how 'active' the resource item is: how much help will it give the student in learning the information/content skill element it contains?

If the system can meet these requirements, a user can, in effect, pre-select likely items, which is important to minimise for him the frustration of finding something is unsuitable — or worse still not realising it and just copying without comprehension. It also overcomes to some extent the difficulty that many items (eg tapes) are not easily 'browsable' and one can waste quite a lot of time fiddling before being able to decide whether to use or reject them.

We may as well say now that constructing such an index is not nearly so fearsome a task as it sounds — it is a matter of pure common sense, not the 'mystical' operation some resource organisers make out, and you can build it up gradually as you have time (for example by pulling out and indexing information you need for a particular project). Nor does it mean you need to have all the items physically to hand all the time. Furthermore its advantages are enormous if you are individualising work.

(1) If it is properly done, you (and your successors at

secondhand) will have a very clear notion of what is available to the students in your subject area and at what levels of difficulty. You will, just by compiling it, or looking through one someone else has compiled, be fulfilling one of the first requirements of individualising learning – KNOWING EXACTLY WHAT IS AVAILABLE.

(2) At any given time you can quickly sort out and collect all relevant items (eg for a project) and you will know what you have got. If you send your students to look in the library or at a 'resource' in the neighbourhood (eg a group of buildings) you can do so in the confidence that unless someone has borrowed it (always a hazard with library items) they will find relevant information where you tell them.

(3) You can capitalise on development of learning skills by getting your students to search out information sources, summarise them and thus extend your index as well!

Information indexing – a method

We suggest that to fulfil your needs, the information index needs to be in two parts: a DESCRIPTIVE document for each item which tells a reader about it, and which is filed by *title* in alphabetical order (but forget words like 'A' or 'The'); a TOPIC index which lists on cards the topics or small subject areas you think students may want to know about and which is filed alphabetically under topic headings. Both will also need *location references*, but ideas on how to produce these are given under 'RETRIEVAL' (page 113).

1. The DESCRIPTIVE document of an item

(a) acts as a stock record for checking

(b) gives an index user basic information about item contents.

For a complex item it can be a card as shown under (iii) on page 109. For a simple item (eg. a single slide) it can be an entry in a register if you don't want to make out a card. In either case it should, as appropriate, include:

— details of its source
— a description of contents sufficiently detailed to give a clear idea of what it contains
— an indication of the sort of people who might find it useful (which can also give you an indication of whom it is *not* suitable for)
— a list of the *topics* for which you think it would be genuinely useful (ie, a *major* source of information)
— a *location reference* (see page 117).

You will see that in order to do this you have to study the resource items and thus get to know them: it will also act as an aide-mémoire for you or your successors at any later date. (You can also put user comments on the back if you want informal opinions!)

2. The TOPIC index (see specimen cards (i) and (ii) opposite). This is, typically, a set of cards, each containing the 'title' or keyword of a topic and brief information on one or more resource items relating to that topic. You can either use one small card per item (which means that the user has to look through a number of cards but gives you plenty of space) or put all items relating to that topic on the same card (which restricts what you can put on it but gives an immediate overview of everything available on the topic). We prefer the second one since it is easier for a user and at the same time gives the index compiler a clear warning of any tendencies to 'hoard'. When the card is full it is usually time to see either if the *topic* is too big and needs to be split or if the collection of items on that topic needs 'weeding' — are any out of date or replaced by something better? It also, after a while, means that the organiser simply has to add a line to a card in most cases rather than make out a new card each time.

In either case the card *heading* is best produced by taking the lists of topics from each resource item descriptive document as you complete it, so that the two parts of the index are always complementary. It means that the list of topic headings will to some extent reflect the personal views of you and your students but is far simpler than trying to use some fixed set of rules and therefore makes less work.

SPECIMEN CARDS FOR A USER-ORIENTED INDEX
County Programmed Learning Centre St Albans

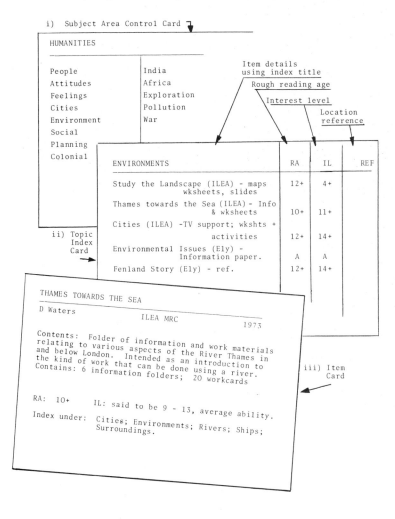

i) Subject Area Control Card

HUMANITIES

People	India
Attitudes	Africa
Feelings	Exploration
Cities	Pollution
Environment	War
Social	
Planning	
Colonial	

Item details
using index title

Rough reading age

Interest level

Location
reference

ii) Topic
    Index
    Card

ENVIRONMENTS	RA	IL	REF
Study the Landscape (ILEA) - maps wksheets, slides	12+	4+	
Thames towards the Sea (ILEA) - Info & wksheets	10+	11+	
Cities (ILEA) -TV support; wkshts + activities	12+	14+	
Environmental Issues (Ely) - Information paper.	A	A	
Fenland Story (Ely) - ref.	12+	14+	

THAMES TOWARDS THE SEA

D Waters

ILEA MRC
1973

Contents: Folder of information and work materials
relating to various aspects of the River Thames in
and below London. Intended as an introduction to
the kind of work that can be done using a river.
Contains: 6 information folders; 20 workcards

iii) Item
     Card

RA: 10+   IL: said to be 9 - 13, average ability.

Index under: Cities; Environments; Rivers; Ships;
              Surroundings.

The *card entry* (see specimen (ii)) should contain

- the short title of the item as on the descriptive card heading (this enables a user to refer to that if he wants to)
- any indication of level of difficulty you want the user to see. (It may be straight — eg, RA (reading age) — 9-10 or more neutral.) For example, a colour code for various ability/attainment levels — '1st year' to indicate it is intended for average first year pupils . . . the details are up to you
- the location reference of the item (see page 117).

It is also desirable to provide for a user looking for broad categories of subject matter and so we suggest that at intervals *subject control cards* (see specimen (i)) should be inserted listing all the topics in that area on which information is available. This may be useful to a student in sorting out exactly what he wants and, if it is only built up as the collection grows, he will be sure of finding something on the topic he chooses.

Note that, apart from this, cross-referencing is not desirable. It is better for the user if you make a full entry on each of the topic cards indicated by your list.

To help you: at the end of this section is a series of procedural guides to reviewing resource items and to indexing, storing and retrieving them. Appendix 1 (the bibliography) is in the form of a section of an information index.

Storage
If you have any quantity of resource items in your possession, whether in a single classroom, a stockroom or a departmental or section 'base', you need to be able to store them so that they will be preserved from damage and so that you can lay your hands on any particular item when you need it. This in turn implies you need to be able to avoid muddle by being able to return items easily and you also need to be able to check periodically if you have lost anything.

There are many specialised forms of storage available but this is written for the classroom teacher and you may have to improvise: we suggest you use the minimum variety of storage places, as under, (see diagram overleaf).

SHELVABLE (open shelves or cupboards): most items such as books, ring binders, boxed kits; you can also shelve others such as pamphlets (in cut-away boxes), slides (in ring binders), tapes and records (in racks), equipment, filmstrips in boxes
FILABLE (vertically in cabinets): individual or groups of paper sheets up to about A4 or larger if folded, slides in special wallets, ohp transparencies, photographs and pictures
FILABLE (flat): similar size: piles of paper such as worksheets, large flat books
OUTSIZE FILE (flat or vertical): *large size* (maps, charts, posters, etc), paper

The two most awkward categories are those which need to be filed flat or which are outsize.

(1) Those items up to about A4 size can be put in nests of trays or nests of cardboard boxes if these are available. If not, you may need to improvise narrow shelving – either by putting shelves close together and dividing them or by, for example, turning a wire mesh shoe rack on its side.

(2) Large maps and charts are always a nuisance: three possible ways suggest themselves.
(i) *Map drawers* if available: these have the advantage of storing items flat but the disadvantage that to make economic use you need to put a lot of items in each drawer. This can be alleviated by making up crude folders or clips to hold about half-a-dozen items each.
(ii) Making up special units to store
(a) flat but vertical – a sort of super-size filing cabinet. The usual one is a frame of wood or metal with bars across the top from which charts, etc, can be hung by eyelets or clips. It keeps the items flat but is unwieldy and they may get damaged when being taken or replaced.

STORAGE FORMS

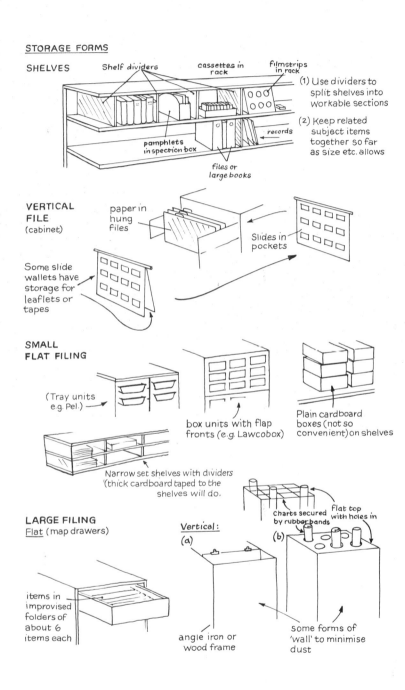

SHELVES

Shelf dividers

cassettes in rack

filmstrips in rack

(1) Use dividers to split shelves into workable sections

(2) Keep related subject items together so far as size etc. allows

records

pamphlets in spection box

files or large books

VERTICAL FILE (cabinet)

paper in hung files

Slides in pockets

Some slide wallets have storage for leaflets or tapes

SMALL FLAT FILING

(Tray units e.g. Pel.)

box units with flap fronts (e.g. Lawcobox)

Plain cardboard boxes (not so convenient) on shelves

Narrow set shelves with dividers '(thick cardboard taped to the shelves will do.

LARGE FILING
Flat (map drawers)

Charts secured by rubber bands

flat top with holes in

Vertical:

(a)

(b)

items in improvised folders of about 6 items each

angle iron or wood frame

some forms of 'wall' to minimise dust

(b) Rolled, horizontally in 'pigeonholes' or vertically in a unit fitted with either a solid top pierced by holes or with a top formed from a wire or batten grid. The main disadvantage is that the item has to be rolled and unrolled each time it is used, so that it may not lie flat and can be damaged.

Choice of this particular type of storage probably depends on how you intend the items to be handled — by teachers alone (eg, for display) or by the students as primary information sources. There is no one right answer. In practice you are probably best off with a lot of shelves or cupboards and a filing cabinet. Desirable extras would be a unit for flat storage of bulk paper and a chart holder — a vertical one with gridded top is the easiest to improvise.

Retrieval
People agonise over 'retrieval systems' usually because they think of these as indissolubly linked with ways of classifying knowledge. That may be so for librarians and other general organisers who cannot know the whole range of subject matter they are trying to organise but your information has already effectively been sorted out by your index. Now you or your students will know *what* the container of their information is (ie, they have the book title, the slide description, etc). All they need from 'retrieval' is to find the item which may be in 'your' collection, in the school collection, or outside (a bit of a cheat, this, since you are likely to send them first to some guide or assignment in the school). Resource retrieval becomes simple if you remember that in basic terms it is using a label or marking on your index card to enable you to find physically the information container *you* have identified — no more, no less. Its main practical problem is that for space reasons you cannot put on the index card something like 'fourth book along on the second shelf in room 23' and that might in any case be undesirable because you would have to alter the index cards every time you wanted to move the item.

Ideally one gets over this problem by having a symbol system that tells you where any item is in a collection of similar items, and having your collection grouped in one spot preferably with someone to run it and answer queries. You cannot rely on either of these because of the problems of individualised work we have already discussed. What would you see as your main practical problems? We suggest you try to note them down before reading on.

(1) Your 'items' are likely to be scattered: in a library, in one or more rooms you use, outside; and some may not be under your control.

(2) You may want to move items from room to room to suit the work.

(3) You want the whole thing to be as little work for you as possible once you have set the system up — after all it is only ancillary to your main job.

So you probably need a compromise whereby an index user can find a label on the card (eg, S1—10 indicates slides 1—10 in the collection), can then look near the index for a 'map' which shows where those slides are to be found at that time, and can go to the place which he can identify by its label. (See page 115(i)). The big advantage for you is that you can move groups of items from room to room without having to alter the index: you just change the map which is much simpler!

This procedure is known as 'notional location referencing' (well, all right, we have just coined the term but it sounds impressive and means what it says so let's adopt it, shall we?) and to fulfil condition (1) above it might well be linked with another labour-saving device known as coarse filing — a concept which has much in common with coarse fishing, coarse sailing, etc, in that it can be practised with reasonable success by rank amateurs although their procedure may horrify the purists.

So what is coarse filing? It is a simple concept using the fact that all resource filing is based on the idea of successive approximations — of moving into a particular location by stages. You approximate when you use a library for example. The catalogue says you will find what you want at Dewey number 736.2, so you look for a set of shelves labelled

RETRIEVAL

(i)

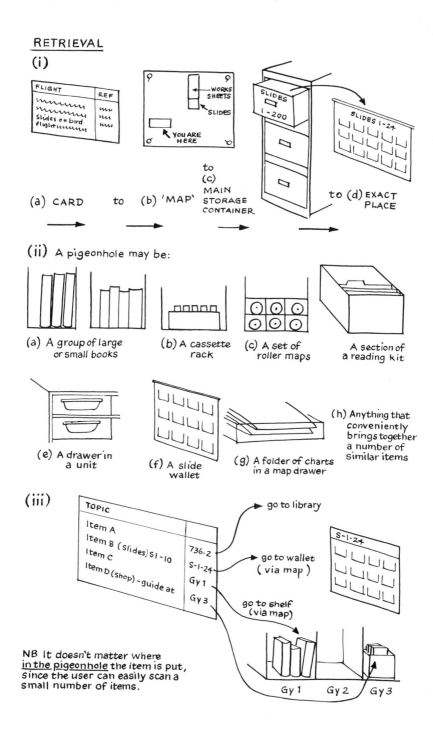

FLIGHT	REF
~~	~~
~~	~~
Slides on bird	~~
flight~~~~~~	~~

WORKS SHEETS
SLIDES
YOU ARE HERE

SLIDES 1-200

to (c) MAIN STORAGE CONTAINER

SLIDES 1-24

(a) CARD   to   (b) 'MAP'   to (d) EXACT PLACE

(ii) A pigeonhole may be:

(a) A group of large or small books

(b) A cassette rack

(c) A set of roller maps

A section of a reading kit

(e) A drawer in a unit

(f) A slide wallet

(g) A folder of charts in a map drawer

(h) Anything that conveniently brings together a number of similar items

(iii)

TOPIC	
Item A	
Item B (slides) S1-10	736.2
Item C	S-1-24
Item D (shop)-guide at	Gy1
	Gy3

go to library

go to wallet (via map)

S-1-24

go to shelf (via map)

Gy1   Gy2   Gy3

NB It doesn't matter where <u>in the pigeonhole</u> the item is put, since the user can easily scan a small number of items.

'700s', then look to find the shelf labelled 730, then look along it to find the books with 736 on them, then find those with 736.2, then find the title you want. With familiarity you may short-circuit the system but the principle remains.

Fine approximations of this kind however, have two disadvantages for the harassed teacher: you must keep individual items in exact order which is time consuming, sometimes makes storage awkward and may mean moving parts of the collection about frequently to make room for new items; and also, it is easy for items to become displaced which either frustrates a student or defeats the object of the final approximation exercise.

Coarse filing argues, therefore:

(1) why not drop the final one or two approximations? It is very little trouble for a user to locate one item physically among, say, twelve big similar ones or twice that number of small ones (eg, slides in a wallet) provided they are clearly compartmented.

(2) Why not take advantage of this – and a good index – to reduce the problems of constantly re-ordering the collection to take in new items?

If you 'pigeonhole' similar items in small groups you can do both these things because you can put similar items together. You let users identify only the broad pigeonhole and then 'search' for the exact item so that it can be put anywhere in the pigeonhole that is convenient – exact item order is no longer important. The only problem is that it may restrict browsing because although you can group items by related content to some extent, it is their shape, size, etc, that is most important if you want to take full advantage of the idea. (See page 115(ii)).

We suggest that in an individualised learning situation, browsability is not important, particularly as regards your own permanent collection of materials. Let students browse at the index where all the 'information about information' is in one place. After all, if *they* can find what they want then you and your successors can too, and that was one of the reasons for making the index in the first place.

So coarse filing works best with pigeonholing and a good index and gives you a quick and easy way to obtain items if combined with notional location referencing.

Location referencing, if you remember among all this pseudo science, simply means devising labels or symbols to enable you to find an item (information container): they appear on the index card, on 'maps', on the items and on any pigeonholes. There are three main types, one of which is peculiar to coarse filing.

(1) 'Library classification' type (eg, the numbers of the Dewey Decimal Classification).

(2) Use of stock control ciphers – typically an accession number system in which items are simply given numbers in order of acquisition (eg, S25 is the twenty-fifth slide you obtained).

(3) Pigeonhole numbering where the locator simply indicates the *pigeonhole* (eg, P1) and all items in that pigeonhole bear that symbol.

Most general resource organisers do not like using what they call 'mixed systems', but then they tend to have central collections and people with nothing to do but organise them. For a teacher who wants quick information retrieval they can be a positive advantage and we suggest you mix all three as needed to achieve your purposes with the least amount of effort.

Think of your index entries (the book titles, etc,) in three groups.

(a) Those referring to items held in the school library/ resource centre but which you may want your students to use: simply use the location reference system used by the library (usually Dewey 'numbers') for *these items only.* Thus a 'library mark' (eg, 736.2) will automatically show the user that the item he wants is in the library (and the library has plenty of ways of finding it for him once he goes there!).

(b) Small items in your collection filed in accession number order (eg, slides) for which you simply use the accession numbers and prefixes as locators in conjunction with a map.

(c)   Larger items (eg, books, tapes) labelled according to their pigeonhole and used in conjunction with a map.

You might want to direct students to outside features direct (eg, a local building) and could then simply write it on the card ('Local nineteenth-century shops, 16—18 High Street'); but you are more likely to direct them first to a detailed index card or another paper item (page 115(iii)) which would act as a learning guide.

This leaves us with the question of what system you use to label the pigeonholes of your own collection, and this is where the 'notional' bit comes in. The less constricting the reference the easier it is to move things around, but in any case it is probably best for you to devise a system to suit your circumstances.

You might, for example,

(a)   label pigeonholes from 1 upwards, irrespective of place, format, etc, so that you might for instance have 1—20, 65—82 as shelf pigeonholes; 21—30 as boxes . . . a modification of this is to use a subject prefix (eg, Gy for geography) to avoid too long a sequence of numbers

(b)   label them with numbers from 1 upwards in series depending on type of *storage* (eg, Sh = shelf 1—2, FC = filing cabinet 1—4 (or whatever)

(c)   label them ditto but using the format of the basic item as a prefix (eg, S for slide, FS for filmstrip) — the snag is you cannot really then use the same prefix for individual items unless you use the 'range' (eg, S1 — 24) to mark the pigeonhole and that is a little cumbersome

(d)   use any natural pigeonholes in addition that you can think of (eg, an SRA reading kit box can simply have 'SRA2a' as its reference and be noted as such on the map since it is big enough to be found easily. The vital thing is to have your map by the index clear so that the code — whatever it is — can be easily broken by the user. (See page 119(a)).

(a)

Map showing location of items, using whatever code you can put on the index cards

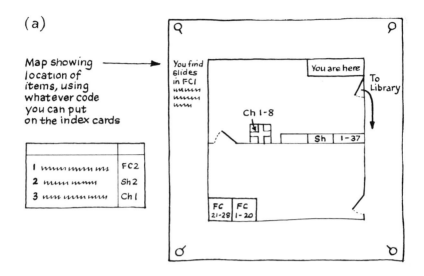

1 ꙍꙍꙍꙍ	FC2
2 ꙍꙍꙍ	Sh2
3 ꙍꙍꙍ	Ch1

Within the map:

You find slides in FC1 ꙍꙍꙍ

You are here

To Library

Ch 1-8

Sh 1-37

FC 21-28 | FC 1-20

(b)

Short title for identification →

Cross out lost or withdrawn titles →

Add items as you put them in →

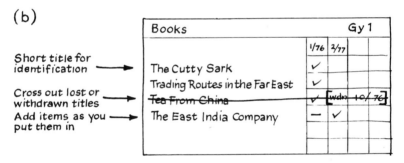

Books			1/76	2/77		
The Cutty Sark			✓			Gy 1
Trading Routes in the Far East			✓			
~~Tea From China~~			✓	[wdn 10/76]		
The East India Company			—	✓		

(c)

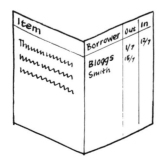

Item	Borrower	Out	In
ꙍꙍꙍ ꙍꙍꙍ ꙍꙍꙍ	Bloggs Smith	1/7 15/1	12/7

OR

BLOGGS, R		2B
ꙍꙍꙍ ꙍꙍꙍ ꙍꙍꙍ	2/7	
ꙍꙍꙍ ꙍꙍꙍ	2/7	3/7

There are also two refinements to retrieval which you may or may not want to bother about.

1. STOCK CONTROL. How do you know if you have lost anything? In practice your descriptive documents and, if you keep one, your accessions register for small items will let you check up, provided they include the item location references. Better still, if you have time, is simply to keep a contents list of each pigeonhole on cards or looseleaf paper (see page 119(b)) which enables you to check the collection a bit at a time when you have a moment to spare (ie, you can take three or four pigeonholes only). It is another chore to start off with but makes the dreary annual stock check much easier.

2. LOAN CONTROL. This is not very likely to be important but if you do lend students items to take away you may want to keep a check. There are various ways – see bibliography – but the simplest is probably to keep a book in which students just write down what they take, when they take it and when they bring it back. Its disadvantage is that you may have to plough through several pages to find an item. Alternatively give each student a card to himself on which loans, etc, are recorded. Libraries have various ticketing systems also to show whether items are 'out' or 'in' but you are not likely to need these: indeed a good principle is not to lend more than you can help and keep the loans short. In individualised learning the student should be needing the item only for a specific piece of work in any case (see page 119(c)).

Display

The third part of organising resources for use is that concerned with making use of the learning base or classroom, showing resource items to

– stimulate interest
– provide feedback for students on their work – 'job satisfaction', so to speak
– provide information where it is convenient
– route and guide students to what one might call 'active' storage – eg, sets of worksheets, check-tests, a bank of

resource items in use, to enable them to select items suitable to their stage of ability and attainment.

There is a tradition in 'classroom display' that the brighter it is and the more varied the better it must be — possibly stemming from the nature of much primary school work where visual presentation of results (eg, measuring objects for relative size) is acknowledged as important. We would suggest that in a genuine individualised learning situation this is not necessarily so and that any 'display' should always be up-to-date and concerned either with work in progress or with preparation for future work. Ask yourself the following questions.

(1) Is it relevant to what is going on at present? We all have a strong temptation, once we have made the effort, to leave a display standing because it took so much work and looks attractive; if, however, it is not relevant to present work or designed to stimulate interest for the future it soon becomes so much wallpaper from the learning point of view: like background music which just avoids silence, it stops one seeing bare walls — and like background music it can become counter-productive if it starts to distract students.

(2) Is it intended to be pre-packaged or are you expecting the students to contribute to the resource display as work goes on?

(3) If it is relevant, is there the *right amount* and what is it *designed to do* — ie, what function is it likely to play in the learning? Much classroom 'decoration' was conceived with the idea of stimulating interest in general but there is some evidence to show that one can over-stimulate — so flood the environment with information that some students can become confused.

This section cannot give detailed guidance on display techniques — look in the bibliography for appropriate books. It simply sets up a series of questions for you to ask yourself once you have decided the function(s) of what you are displaying.

Stimulating interest

(1) Do you want to stimulate interest without necessarily wanting to guide the student to a particular goal (a display of reading books is an example?

You may well need a wide variety of material and are likely to keep changing individual items in a basic long-term display: but make sure the long-term display does not just become 'part of the furniture' and lose its point.

(2) Do you want to stimulate interest with a particular goal in mind − ie, to guide the student towards a particular topic/item/process or one of a selection of such things?

You will need to change the display as your intention changes and are likely to need a short-term display, easily altered or packed up altogether. DO YOU KNOW WHAT IS AVAILABLE?

Providing feedback to students

(3) Do you want the students to 'build up' the display themselves as the work goes on − progressive feedback mainly for their own benefit − or do you want them to do it at the end so as to gain satisfaction from showing others what they have done?

Provide information (eg, in a project)

(4) *Why* do you want to provide information in this way? *What* information do you consider better provided in this way than by other means?

This is likely to be very topical and short lived − we suggest you could use news clippings; information researched by students and useful to others; large chart type displays likely to be frequently referred to; commonly used pictures and other aids as part of a constantly changing information 'board' − change it to ensure as far as possible that students get into the habit of looking to see what is new.

Routing and guiding

(5) What are you wanting to do:

(a)   guide them to a particular place or item (eg, worksheet holder; a reading kit)?

(b)   take them through a series of items (a sequence of pictures)?

(c)   show them how to do something simple?

A checklist for examining resource items 1. What is the title? 2. What are the general contents (a rough description of what the item contains)?	
3. Can you list (a) the subject topics which you think would be useful with the chapter, page references etc?	
(b) the level of difficulty (for an average pupil)? (eg, 1st year sec.)	
(c) If it would be useful for others (eg, remedial 3rd yr. primary)	
(d) level of interest if you feel this is important.	
4. Does it have help for students built in (eg, tests) or separately (eg, assignment cards)? If so, what?	
5. What is the FORMAT (books; slides; it; etc)?	
6. Can it be split up for use by more than 1 person? Do you have several copies? If so, how many?	
7. Can it be 'browsed' or does the user need special equipment?	

Suggested review slip (if checklist made re-usable)

Title:

Contents:	Topic:	

Level of difficulty:

Level of interest:

*Ancillary material available

*Format
*No of people who can use it:
*No of copies:

*This is teacher-information and you can note it on the
back of your descriptive cards if desired.

(1)

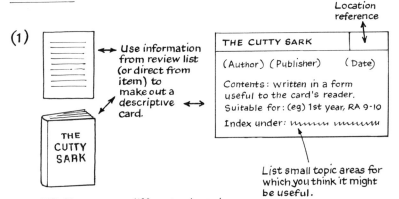

Location reference

⟵ Use information from review list (or direct from item) to make out a descriptive card. ⟶

THE CUTTY SARK

THE CUTTY SARK

(Author) (Publisher)   (Date)

Contents: written in a form useful to the card's reader.
Suitable for: (eg) 1st year, RA 9-10

Index under: ~~~~~ ~~~~~~

List small topic areas for which you think it might be useful.

NB You can use different coloured cards EITHER to show <u>where</u> the item is (eg, red for library, white for your own collection) OR to show that special equipment is needed for its use (eg, blue for tape-based).

(2)

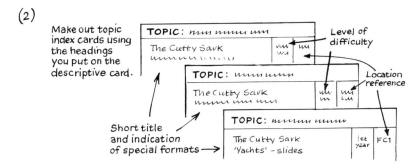

Make out topic index cards using the headings you put on the descriptive card.

TOPIC: ~~~ ~~~~ ~~~

Level of difficulty

The Cutty Sark
~~~~~ ~ ~~~~

TOPIC: ~~~~ ~~~~

Location reference

The Cutty Sark
~~~~ ~~~ ~~~

Short title and indication of special formats ⟶

TOPIC: ~~~~~ ~~~~~

The Cutty Sark
'Yachts' – slides   1st year   FC1

(3)   Enter topic headings on any control cards if you think it necessary. Put them alphabetically in the <u>topic index</u> among the topic cards.

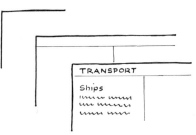

TRANSPORT

Ships
~~~~ ~~~~
~~~ ~~~~
~~~~ ~~~

(4)   Keep both sets of cards in separate boxes, filed alphabetically.

(1) Store items in pigeonholes by shape/size
(using prefixes as desired.)

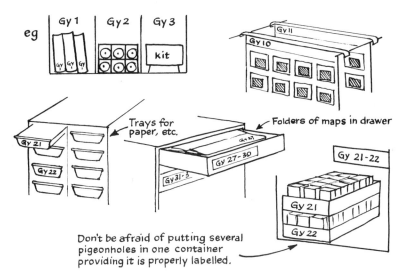

Trays for paper, etc.

Folders of maps in drawer

Don't be afraid of putting several
pigeonholes in one container
providing it is properly labelled.

OR

(2) Pigeonhole as above but with prefixes indicating type of storage.
eg, B for basic (books and items such as kits, roller maps, that
can be stored like books); S for slides, which need a special type
of storage; D for drawers (for things such as maps and charts).

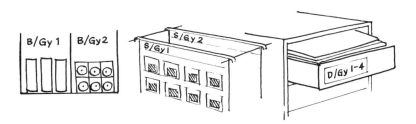

NB Big departments must decide whether to have one omnibus prefix
(eg, 'Gy' to combine 'Geography' and 'Geology', 'Sc' for all science)
or to split to indications of subject (eg, 'Cy'– Chemistry , 'By'– Biology)

Service collections by

(1) Entering new items

 — make out a descriptive
  index card and decide on
  TOPICS and SUITABILITY and
  LOCATION (pigeonhole).

 — enter on appropriate topic
  cards, and pigeonhole no. —
  (make out new topic card
  if needed.)

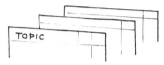

 — enter on appropriate
  pigeonhole list by short title.

 — put pigeonhole label on item
  and put item in pigeonhole.

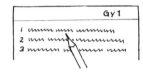

(2) Periodic checks

 — check individual pigeonholes
  as and when convenient,
  using contents cards.

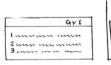

 — check and modify maps, etc,
  if items/pigeonholes are
  removed.

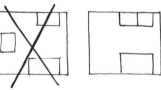

(3) Withdraw or cancel lost or worn-out items

 — find descriptive card and withdraw or cancel it

 — from entry on descriptive card locate
  appropriate topic cards and cross
  out item.

 — from entry on descriptive card
  locate appropriate pigeonhole
  contents list and delete item.

(4) As situation arises

If a TOPIC CARD becomes full, review items to see if any are no
longer needed. This can indicate a need to 'weed' the collection.

8. Designing student work materials

General aims
This chapter sets out to help you implement individual
assignments by producing guides to modifying and creating
resource materials. It does *not* teach you the minutiae of
writing or scripting but should alert you to the characteristics
all work materials must have.

Goals
When you have worked through it you should, with some
practice, be able to

— identify general problems in the design of student work
  materials
— identify possible functions of such materials
— identify possible formats for such materials
— identify the media characteristics of such materials and
  their effects on material design and use
— select appropriate media and formats for a given learning
  assignment
— identify various structuring problems in designing
  materials, *viz* providing instructions; procedures; questions;
  feedback.

The chapter is in six sections.

1. General problems (p 130)
2. Characteristics of student materials (p 134)
3. Formats and media characteristics of materials (p 143)
4. Structuring problems of student materials (p 152)
5. An algorithm for determining format and medium (p 165)
6. A check diagram for use in constructing materials (p 176)

This chapter poses something of a dilemma since the design
and production of student work materials is central to any
successful individualised or resource oriented work. At the
same time the book is only a guide and so can only discuss
the problems, not give detailed instructions.

There are, essentially, two sets of problems:

(1)   those inherent in the learning process itself
(2)   those which we, as teachers, impose because of our
        training and our real or imagined capabilities as authors.

The first part of this chapter discusses these general problems briefly; the second part offers some suggestions to help you surmount them.

General problems
Learning or work materials tend to be designed at the single assignment level because they translate to the student what you intend him to do, and then help or teach him as you think desirable. To produce successful materials you will need to have already:

(1)   worked out, with or without your students' agreement, the general goals: you will be clear *what* you want achieved and *how* you want it achieved in general terms
(2)   accepted that, except where you deliberately write-in 'referrals', the student should be able to carry out the assignment by using only the material you provide together with any other information or tools it refers him to. He will need to be able to interact with the material in the same way that you would expect him to interact with your teaching.

The first, we hope, is achievable; the second requirement is your main problem because the student will usually be engaged in active learning and active learning implies not just reception of ideas, knowledge, etc, but querying, investigation, manipulation of them. In teaching, you as the teacher are central to this process, interposing yourself as the interpreter or mediator. (See A opposite.) The more you become concerned with individualised or resource-oriented work the more you inevitably move out to the side, into a managing, guiding or monitoring position. So the diagram of learning interaction, instead of being A, becomes more like B, C or D. In producing student materials this makes things more difficult because of the fact that most 'resources' are passive by nature. They do not positively help the student to learn

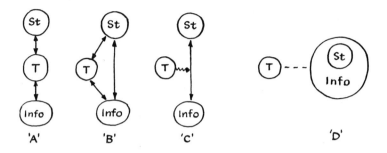

but need interpreting. Hence if you are going to remove the direct intervention of the teacher you need to replace it with some other mediator which will 'activate' the sources on which the student works, or will actively facilitate his performance of a learning assignment. Thus the material will need to

- be appropriate to *what* you want the student to do – both in how it gets him to learn and in the level of difficulty it presents
- make as much use of existing resources as possible, both to save your preparation time and to provide a variety of work for the student.

Unfortunately these requirements often become obscured because of our self-imposed problems. Perhaps because there is an element of creativity in most of us, we tend to think that there is little problem in writing and planning materials – hence the oft-heard cries of 'What are we supposed to be doing, Miss?' or 'Ah, but I didn't really mean that' as another student fails inexplicably to comprehend material we thought was crystal clear. Indeed it is a salutary thought that *you* might be doing just that at this moment.

Now one of the troubles about designing student learning materials is that there is no one right way of doing it. Most teachers probably have the feeling that they are 'authors manqués' and can *of course* produce elegant and clear work. Yet you might like to pause for a moment: publishers accept three general 'levels' of authorship development:

— *making anthologies*, in which all the author does is select items of other people's work that interest him, and group them together with a few comments

— *compilation*, in which the author largely takes ideas, facts, etc, from others but, to some extent, makes them his own by rephrasing, synthesising, interpreting and discussing them

— *creation*, in which the author expresses his own thoughts, views, ideas in his own way — quite possibly, indeed, basing them on previous works since very little thought now is truly original but making them very much his own.

Many work materials get no further than anthologising or, at best, the early stages of compilation since the task becomes more difficult and time consuming as an author goes 'up'; because it gets more difficult, it does not necessarily produce better material. This little book is, hopefully, somewhere between compilation and creation but that does not necessarily mean that it is either superbly clear, or that it does better what may already have been done before.

The more one tries to synthesise and develop ideas, the more danger there is of obscuring them; yet just to collect or anthologise may not be enough or be appropriate to what one is trying to achieve. We can, with the very best intentions, easily produce material that does not help the student and can even interfere with the learning because of our lack of authorship skills.

Secondly, we may well approach the design of student material with preconceived notions of what it 'should' be like. Most people tend to visualise material by its form and medium — you think of it as 'an assignment card', 'a worksheet', 'a slide-tape programme', and examples of these that you have seen tend to determine how you design your own material: yet these patterns can in themselves be deceptive. It's comparatively simple to get people to make *technically* competent forms of material; that is to make neat, professional-looking worksheets with elegant artwork; audio-visual presentations that have excellent sound quality, well-exposed and attractive visuals. Yet if there is little or no thought given to the learning characteristics the materials can be virtually useless because there are no clear goals, or because they are inappropriate to what you want the student to achieve. Worse, just as in teaching, a bad piece of material can positively interfere with the work and can even de-motivate the student.

To sum up, just to 'translate' your own teaching or lecturing into a 'self-sufficient' form may not be enough because the flexibility inherent in teaching has gone and you can no longer guarantee to be there to:

(1) stimulate and, if need be, re-motivate the student
(2) reply to queries or identify problems which the student may not recognise.

In a sense, the problem of this chapter is a paradigm of the problem of designing learning material itself. It might be fairly easy to give 'rules' for producing, say, a worksheet to carry out a particular learning task, but those rules might not transfer to the design of other types of material. To produce a generalised guide may be more useful in the long run because it can be applied to a variety of situations – but it will not instruct you in the minutiae of designing specific materials which you may need now. All one can do is to provide the guidance framework which you can use to build on and let you make the decisions and use your own skills to put 'flesh on the bones'.

The guide which follows is in two parts which might be described as:

(1) how to ensure your material will be appropriate – will have all the features needed to enable the student to be successful
(2) a consideration of the problems of incorporating those features in your actual 'writing' of the material (in which we include design of visual elements, etc).

It can be read straight through but will probably be most useful to you if you have a student task in mind and follow that through.

It should be noted here that there are two ways to produce

student work material:

(a) *intuitively,* but only you know if you can do this so that the requirements stated at the beginning of this chapter are fulfilled. If you can (sure ?) you don't need help. If you can't we cannot help you to do so.

(b) *by careful planning*: this is the way the guide will suggest. It does mean putting aside preconceptions for the moment and having a clear idea of WHAT is to be done and WHY you want the student to do it.

Characteristics of student materials

This section should enable you to identify the structural elements of various types of work material and to select those necessary to enable the student to complete a given learning task. These elements are:

(1) what job the material is intended to do in general (its teaching function)

(2) how you are going to present it to the student — its format 'shape' and the medium of presentation

(3) the teaching structure you need to build in to enable the assignment material to do what you would otherwise have done — the interpretation and guidance element.

(2) and (3) depend on (1), and (1) in turn depends on what you have found out about goals, learning skills available or needing developing, reasons for the learning taking place. (2) also depends on the available resources — or the means of producing anything you want which is not readily available. Furthermore, we have indicated earlier that, to some extent at least, an individualised assignment takes the place of the teacher while the student(s) are working on it. If you accept this, it follows that the assignment must incorporate the 'learning management' characteristics of a teacher, or at least those which you decide are appropriate. Specifically . . .

(1) It has within it, somewhere, three elements:

(a) *instructions* — telling, urging, suggesting to the student what to do and possibly how to do it: these might be provided by the teacher or by the student material

(b) *stimulus material* — the content or information on which the student is going to work: it might be part of the student material or be provided by other resource items

(c) *indicators of results* — ways of showing how the student is getting on in applying the instructions: these are, in effect, his observable responses and the progress they show.

As an analogy in normal teaching, the teacher may explain something to a class (stimulus material), ask questions about it (instructions) and assess the answers or *responses* he gets to see if the class has grasped his explanation. You need to distinguish all these in writing assignments since you need to identify whether they are included within the material you produce *or are contained in other resource items.*

(2) It needs 'mechanisms' to replace the teacher's mediation function, his interpretation and control of the learning task. Typically these might be provided by:

— directions
— questions
— feedback devices
— controls on student pacing and other factors.

Which you use, how often and in what way depends on what you want the *material* to do and how it is to be presented to the student. The function you envisage for the material is clearly the most important characteristic so let us look at that first.

NOTE: The six pages following are in the form of simplified *information maps*. The principle is exactly that of an atlas — the ability to separate and display separate aspects of a piece of subject matter so that they can be studied (a) alone, (b) in comparison with other aspects. Thus one can have general maps which give superficial information about a whole country and detailed maps which give specific information — the level.

The advantages claimed for information mapping are that it helps to classify one's thoughts and makes retrieval of specific items of information very easy. The corresponding disadvantages are that one has to analyse the information content very clearly to produce such maps and that the format may be restricting (like an atlas, a general rule is that each 'map' should not spill over to more than one page.

Resource-oriented work   *Functions of material*
Design of student materials   *Overview*

Introduction: student work material may be designed to fulfil one or more of five main *functions*.

It may:
— stimulate: raise interest and/or provoke reactions
— direct or instruct: tell a student what to do (without helping) or give him instructions as to how to do it
— guide: help a student to develop his own learning
— teach: teach a student something he did not know or could not do beforehand
— give practice: help a student consolidate his work

Each of these functions imparts certain characteristics to student work material and so they need to be clearly identified.

Contents: the following pages each contain a description of one function, its uses, characteristics and problems. They are arranged in a standard format so that you can make quick comparisons.

Resource-oriented work   *Functions of material*
Design of student materials   *Materials to stimulate*

Uses: to raise interest or provoke reactions.

Characteristics: they provide ideas and information but without giving guidance as to what to do with it or even which parts of it to choose for further development.

Examples: information displays; for example, a display on the classroom wall that can interest students without your intervention, an audio-visual programme designed simply to set students off on any one of a number of courses of action, interest-whetting items deliberately included in other work.

Comment: a danger of using such materials in individualised work is the fallacious idea that simple contact with potentially interesting information will by itself stimulate purposeful learning without further guidance. Stimulation materials always need to be backed up with organised work once the student's interest is caught.

Analogy: in terms of the 'learning map' analogy, these materials are the brochures which catch your interest and make you want to visit a particular place or go over a particular route.

Resource-oriented work   *Functions of material*
Design of student materials   *Directing materials*

Uses: to give a student instructions; to provide ways of overcoming a simple problem it is not desired to *teach* him the answer to.

Characteristics: they do not normally contain guidance but simply direct a student where to go (eg, to find something) or what to do. A variant is the decision-making procedure which actually solves problems for a student without learning necessarily taking place.

Examples: a set of instructions which tell a student to go and find out something, or to carry out a certain task (use an information resource item, use a skill) and to come back with results; instructions incorporating information (eg, a passage of writing with comprehension test questions; a tape which asks a child to listen and then identify sounds).

Comment: whatever its actual format, the major limitation is that the student must have any necessary learning skills *before* he is given material of this type. It should therefore be used only where students are using or reinforcing learning or content skills (practising) or you want them to concentrate on content information while being certain that they can do the tasks you ask. A danger is that teachers often associate 'assignment cards' of this type automatically with 'discovery' learning and either *assume* mastery of the necessary skills or use the material inappropriately.

Analogy: in learning map terms these materials are *route maps.*

Resource-oriented work   *Functions of material*
Design of student materials   *Guiding materials*

Uses: to help a student without actually solving the problem for him; to suggest various lines of development; to take the student over an obstacle which he needs to cross but which is identified as being outside the learning he is currently doing (eg, he may need to make a mathematical computation in order to progress; the material may simply give him the answer).

Characteristics: while not teaching a student they do give him help — clues as to what to do and even, where needed, prompting as to how to do it. They can be developments of 'directing' material in that you still basically ask a student to do something but give him some help along the way by asking questions about particular aspects, by illustrating difficulties or by building-in consultation with the teacher. Alternatively, they can be purpose-built generalised guides which he can use for variations of the same task.

Examples: Question-and-answer sheets referring to specific resource items; worksheets of the type the student completes as he goes from one stimulus item to another; guide procedures such as that on pp 166-175 of this book.

Comment: they are most use where you want the student to (a) develop existing or embryonic content or learning skills so as to increase his mastery of them or extend his range, (b) achieve learning goals of the more complex type, involving formation of concepts, opinions, attitudes, where students do not want to be *told* but where they may need connections pointed out or avenues of exploration indicated. Because of the problems of asking questions and providing the right assistance these are probably the most difficult materials to produce and it is very easy to think you are producing guides when you are either merely 'directing' or are simply producing rote teaching.

Analogy: in learning map terms, we are talking of guide books to that enticing town, or of suggesting ways of overcoming the river barrier. They may even provide stepping stones if we feel that the barrier is irrelevant!

Resource-oriented work   *Functions of material*
Design of student materials   *Teaching materials*

Uses: to teach a student by individualised means.

Characteristics: they should
(a)   have clearly achievable goals with built-in checks on how far the student achieves them
(b)   be designed to do a specific job — either to surmount a particular difficulty or to teach a particular skill, etc
(c)   have content and format appropriate to the task
(d)   be guaranteed to allow the student to achieve the goals with what might be called job satisfaction — if he gets there but hates the process they are not fully successful.

Examples: typically they comprise individual pieces of work in one or more media and often linked together as a series: a sort of embryo structured work scheme. They often include any necessary content information either in a worksheet/ work booklet or in an associated pack.

Comment: depressingly often, also, such materials are repetitive and boring to the student once the novelty has worn off. We may all be potential writers, but the flexible teaching mode, with the instant response and variation provided by a teacher, does not translate easily; once its flexibility is lost, defects we never noticed in our teaching emerge. Before producing such material it is wise to ask if the learning task can be carried out some other way — by group teaching perhaps?

Analogy: in learning map terms, the need should arise when we feel that because of our student's abilities or slow speed, or because the content is generally difficult, we have to build a bridge over that difficult river or actually make a road for the student to follow.

Resource-oriented work   *Functions of material*
Design of student materials   *Practice materials*

Uses: to enable a student to consolidate learning, especially the use of content or learning skills.

Characteristics: they get the student to carry out, over and over again, operations involving use of knowledge or skill he has, or is supposed to have, learnt. They do not teach or guide except incidentally.

Examples: typically they are sheets of paper with a number of similar items on, but can be produced in many forms; practical tasks with instructions to do them; instructions in various media requiring repetitive responses.

Comment: the problems are threefold.
(a) How does the student know at any time whether his practice is successful?
(b) How much practice does he need to have?
(c) How far should the material go? When does the practice become further development?
Their design may well depend on whether what is being practised is essentially a content skill or a learning skill.

Analogy: they may well be thought of as checks to ensure that a student can read a route-map; use a guide to the town, etc.

You may well be saying by this time that the whole thing is a little artificial. 'After all, I rarely use material for one purpose alone . . . it usually combines different functions.' It is certainly true that we often do combine various functions within a single piece of material, but we suggest it is important to identify and isolate each separate function in such a case. There is a very sensible little labour-saving procedure which suggests that you first see if conditions allow you simply to direct a student to materials already in existence. If you can't do that, can you solve the problem by providing guides to existing materials? If you can't do that then you may be able to do it by guides plus some modification of existing material. Only as a last resort should you write your own. So *what* an assignment is intended to achieve for the student may well determine how any material should be constructed.

The *functions* of the material may not affect any medium of presentation but they may well determine its *format*, which we will discuss next.

Formats and student material

What we are calling the format is simply the overall structure into which instructions, resource items, etc, can be incorporated to enable a given set of activities to be carried out. It is based on the fact that individualised work has instructions (I), stimulus material of various kinds (S_1 S_2 S_3, etc) and built-in feedback to give and assess results (R). Given this, there are four basic formats for student work material which equate roughly to the main divisions we listed in the 'Resource organisation' dimensions back in Chapter 1.

(1) Use of instructions to direct student to pieces of stimulus material elsewhere: results may not be clearly identified.

	uses	*equates to*
	to direct	'resource-based'
	to stimulate	

(2) An instructional source (directions, questions, hints) designed to make the student interact constantly with pieces of stimulus material not incorporated in it. Provision is usually made for recording results.

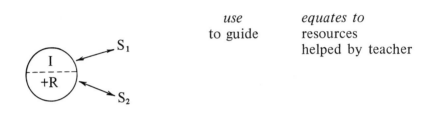

use   *equates to*
to guide   resources
             helped by teacher

(3) A variant of (2) in which the instructional material incorporates some basic stimulus material as a 'springboard' which the student uses to study other materials: it usually provides for feedback and recording results.

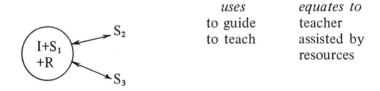

uses   *equates to*
to guide   teacher
to teach   assisted by
              resources

(4) An instructional source built in to the information material. It incorporates feedback and record of results.

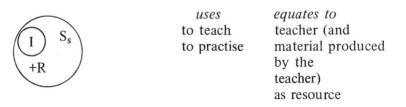

uses   *equates to*
to teach   teacher (and
to practise   material produced
               by the
               teacher)
               as resource

(3) and (4), and more occasionally (2), may either have the results of the students' work incorporated in the instructional material (eg, a worksheet in which the answers to questions are filled in) or they may require the results to be recorded elsewhere (eg, in an exercise book).

In general, format (1) is most useful for stimulating and directing because in order to use it the student needs already to have any necessary learning skills.

Format (2) is very useful for guiding but does make considerable demands on outside resources so it has the problems that it can really only be used by individuals or small groups, or else be one of a number of parallel assignments so that all students do not need to use the same item at one time. The teacher must be very fully conversant with the resource items.

Format (3) is useful in that, by incorporating some basic stimulus information, the teacher at once exercises more control over the learning and can provide a common 'springboard' for a group of students. Again it needs careful organisation to ensure that the outside resources are sufficient.

Format (4) is very common both in practice work and in 'individualised' teaching where a group has to work on the same subject at the same time. It cuts down the requirements for outside resources and gives the teacher considerable control. Many teachers therefore find it very attractive *but* it also has great problems. Because of authorship failings and pressure of work it may well become repetitive and boring. It can also be bad because it tends to lead to the use of 'potted' information and since many of the source books are already 'potted' to some degree, the information is very much diluted by the time it reaches the student. The quality of his learning therefore drops.

We would therefore reiterate that, in resource-oriented work, it is best where possible to use or modify existing information sources rather than try to create 'new' ones.

There are two final points to note.

(1) The more the instructions and stimulus materials are combined   the   more   teacher/authorship   problems

become important and the more likely the activities are to be resource-oriented *teaching* rather than resource-oriented active learning.

(2)   The format as such is not dependent on the use of any particular media. It is a way of organising the material. Thus format (1) could be a sheet of paper bearing instructions to go to certain books; it could equally be an audio-tape telling a student what to do or a list of items to see in a museum.

At the same time format and presentation medium do tend to interact in practice because

(a)   the format you want to fulfil particular functions may lend itself to a particular medium for the sake of convenience, etc

or

(b)   available resource items and their media may to some extent indicate which of several possible formats you decide to use.

Let us therefore have a look at the media characteristics of student materials.

Media characteristics of student work material

The ways of presenting information to the student are many and various – and they raise problems because of the barrage of 'special interests' involved. For example what is your first reaction to the word 'Media'?

The thing that most people consider as 'media' in resource-based or individualised work is what the manufacturers like them to think of – complex equipment which allows attractive if expensive presentations; perhaps they feel it is the nearest thing to a 'live' teacher and the furthest from the often dull (and socially 'discredited'?) textbook. So to many people 'media' equals radio, television, audio-visual devices and materials to put with them; and many people take these as being desirable in themselves, an integral part of the learning process. 'I'm going to teach by the overhead projector', say the media enthusiasts, but they don't really mean it. They may be *teaching* by any of a number of methods – lecture, demonstration, lesson . . . What they are doing with their device is use it as a means of presenting part of the information they use in the teaching process. That may well be very sensible and you *can*, assuredly, use any given medium to help inculcate learning. If you are a real enthusiast for it, and a good teacher, you will succeed – but you are rather in the position of the man who bought a bicycle for getting to work and found that, because of traffic conditions, he got there quicker than by car. He was so pleased that he advocated using the bicycle for everything . . . of course he had to stick spikes on the wheels for climbing slippery slopes and he got wet crossing the river because it didn't float very well even with balloons to add buoyancy . . . well *he* didn't mind because he had convinced himself that the bicycle was the best (and very soon 'the only') means of transport. It was the people he half-sold the idea to who suffered. So you *can* use film loops to teach everything from maths to reading and you *can* put all your teaching on to synchronised tape/slide programmes even if the student has to switch off every two minutes to go and do some work. BUT there is a danger that you may well be attracted to the more complex media because they are attractive and forget that lovely wrapping paper does not always conceal a splendid present. The point is that they are only *carriers* of information and what matters is whether a particular carrier is appropriate or not.

In the long run, there are only two valid reasons for choosing a particular carrier, especially in goal oriented learning.

(a)   The resource item you want to use is available only in that particular medium (eg, you may just have a set of slides on 'rock faults' or whatever) in which case you need to accept whatever demands it makes.

(b)   You think the medium has characteristics that are particularly favourable for facilitating a particular piece of learning – to help the student achieve his goals (eg, a child cannot read fluently: it might help to put the assignment instructions on tape and let him listen instead. You want to encourage creativity and the medium of photography is a way of developing that). A sub-set of this reason is that you feel a particular medium may help motivate the student. It can certainly happen but remember that the motivation induced by the medium will continue only if the learning is successful. If it isn't the interest aroused by the medium will fade. Much worksheet learning suffers from this. The first one is novel and produces a Hawthorne effect. It is not very rewarding, however, so the student is less enthusiastic about the next . . . the third very similar one is 'just another bit of work'!

All of which, you may say, is very interesting but how do we choose? Well, why not forget the hardware for the moment, with all the issues it conjures up, and look at the communication characteristics of what you want to do. Student work material, whatever its nature, usually has two major elements

— the instructional (telling, teaching, guiding)
— the stimulus (information content as displayed to the student).

Likewise the medium or means of presenting these to the students really has two elements.

(1)   The basic 'carrier' which may, in student material be:
— 'paper' — ie, flat, writable-on material
— recorded sound
— live sound (eg, your voice)
— projected visuals (still)
— projected visuals (moving)
— objects (inanimate)
— living things.

Note that (a) we are not talking about particular *devices* but the general carrier medium, (b) these can be combined (eg, a sound film is an example of a mixture of recorded sound and moving visuals) and (c) that for a *student* the characteristics of any particular one may change (eg, an overhead projector transparency, though an example of 'projected still visual' medium can also take on some of the characteristics of 'paper' if laid on a white background since it can then be read without requiring a machine).

(2) The means or code by which the information is conveyed:
- sounds (as sounds)
- words
- diagrams
- pictures (paintings, sketches, photographs, etc)
- symbols
- patterns
- objects
- smells.

Which of these you use may be governed by the work activities you think desirable and by the nature of any appropriate resource items you have available. Unless these raise serious problems, however, they have some innate characteristics which are favourable or otherwise to various carrier media.

As can be seen from page 150, some carriers are better than others at conveying messages in our context (student work material) but you usually do not have 'all other things equal'. You are likely to have certain constraints imposed either by the nature of the learning or by the nature of your resources. Thus you may think it important to have

- ease of use by a student (depending on the activity)
- availability for more than one at a time
- simplicity of production.
- The student may need to have the stimulus always in front of him to work on (ie, it must be permanent not ephemeral to his senses); or he may need to move about with the material (especially if it is directing or guiding him).
- He may need to use resource items not incorporated in the material itself.

So even if you can find several 'carrier' media that convey your message you may still find one (or all of them) may not meet all your requirements and then you need to choose.

(a)

Characteristics of various communication media in relation to information stimuli (from teacher/producer's point of view)

	sounds	words	diagrams	pictures	graphic symbols	patterns	objects	smells
'paper'								
recorded sound		•	•			•		•
live sound		•	•	•	•			•
still protected visual		•	•	•	•	•	•	•
moving projected visual		•		•	•	•	•	•
inanimate objects								
animate objects								

Key

- = good
- = can provide some indication
- = requires equipment to use

(b)

Carrier media with characteristics positively favourable to presenting particular information stimuli

	sounds	words	diagrams	pictures	graphic symbols	patterns	textures	objects	smells	static / ephemeral	ease of production	ease of use	flexibility in use
television	•	•	•	•	•	•	•	•		•	5	2/3	3
*film	•	•						•			5	4	4
*film loop	•	•						•		•	5	2	3
slides											3	2	1
audiotapes										•	2	2/3	2
slides											4	3	4
ohp trps		•	•	•		•					1	1	1
'paper'											1	1	1

Key
still

moving

— good

• = can be used to do this if no other conditions dictate its use (eg, a film can show moving pictures of objects which can show some of their characteristics; television can show static diagrams but it is a cumbersome method!)

* — if *sound* is needed, match with 'audio-tapes'

1–5 scale of difficulty/complexity: higher the number the more difficult/rigid in use

Page 150(a) gives general guidance so long as you remember that most carrier media can be modified (eg, although recorded sound is by nature ephemeral it can be replayed, but that in turn requires some skill and if your requirements were, say, simplicity and a need to have the information constantly displayed you would use it only if the student could not read. On the other hand if you wanted to train him in concentration you might deliberately use recorded sound because it is both ephemeral and can yet be replayed to check).

In practice, if you decide that a particular carrier (eg, recorded sound) is appropriate to your needs you then have to locate the appropriate device — do you use a gramophone or a cassette tape recorder or what? That decision is dictated by

(a)   whatever existing resource items you want to use
(b)   equipment you have
(c)   (for 'new' items) the constraints listed above and any positive benefits the medium may provide.

Page 150(b) tries to sum up the *positive* characteristics of various examples of carrier device in presenting particular messages — and gives some indication of problems in use. If, however, you want to explore the problem in a little more depth we suggest you read the section on *format* and then use the algorithmic procedure provided on p165 to work out what effect format and media factors will have on *your* material design. If you want to go even further please consult the information index on p195.

In all this it is wise to remember that the more complex media are good servants but bad masters. If you need to use available resource items and they are complex, then you will have to adapt your student material to fit their demands. It is, for example, very difficult to modify information conveyed by the more complex media. To edit, say, an existing film is physically difficult and usually politically impossible unless you own it; you therefore have to plan round it if you wish to use such an item. If you have freedom of choice, then let your choice of carrier medium depend on the nature of the learning to be undertaken, as defined by its goals, etc, the most usable format, and any internal structuring needed in the material. To choose the medium first is likely to introduce problems rather than to solve them.

Structuring student work material

Let us start with an analogy. Ensuring that material has appropriate format and presentation characteristics would, we hope you agree, equate with a teacher's overall plan or strategy for a lesson. It provides the vehicle for learning. In the same way in individualised work the detailed structuring of student materials substitutes for the teacher's interpretation and mediation of the learning in a lesson and, just as in lesson planning, there are general principles and detailed techniques which may help to make it effective.

Principles first: structuring of material has, we suggest, four basic elements.

(1) *The actual collection, preparation and organisation of any information stimulus material involved,* either as part of a self-contained 'package' or as outside resource items to be worked on. Here you have to take into account:

> (i) its suitability for the intended students
> — is the verbal level right?
> — is the conceptual level right?
> — what range of students will use it?
> — how easy is it to use?
> (ii) its presentation structure (in terms of information layout)
> — is it clear?
> — is it appropriate to what you want to do?
> (iii) its usefulness for learning
> — how 'active' is it?
> — do you need to make it more active? to modify it in some way?

These are important because any information you deliberately incorporate into an assignment needs to have been considered as to:

WHY you want that particular bit.

WHERE the student will get it from (in the work material, nearby, from an outside source).

HOW, if need be, you are going to adapt it if you identify defects. Is it a matter of changing the level or of changing its nature? (eg, A set of slides may have useless notes because they are too complex; the visuals might be useful for their original purpose if you simplify the notes or they might be useful to incorporate in something entirely different.)

You need to look very carefully at your stimulus material and YOU are the only person who can do that but on the whole the rule we mentioned before is a good one to follow.

(i)   If circumstances allow, direct or guide students to work with existing material.
(ii) Only if it is not suitable consider:
      (a) adapting the material and guiding students to use the result
      (b) producing your own collection of material which can be used for several purposes (different assignments; perhaps various levels with appropriate guidance).
(iii) *Only* as a last resort (or if you have to use it for group teaching) create your own 'self-contained' materials.

Far too many innovations, given the authorship problems, blunder into producing extensive and complicated self-contained materials which often do not meet their needs.

(2)   *The second principle is that of controlling the learning by advance structuring of the material.*
      A teacher can to a large extent control his lesson 'on the spot' because he is there: he can quickly modify an approach, cut out parts to save time, help with problems, even change the whole purpose. In producing *material* you lose much of that flexibility and so you need to decide in advance how far you want to control the student's work and how you are going to do it.

Do you want:

(i) to determine the exact content — in which case you must direct or guide the student to specified information for specified reasons

(ii) to determine in detail his method of work — the more you wish to do this, the more likely you are to produce a self-contained package, with all the problems that implies

(iii) to control the speed of his work (student pacing). This is one of the most difficult problems since people's natural pace of work varies widely and indeed, without controls, any student-oriented task tends to take two or three times as long as it would if you taught it. If you do need to enforce pacing you may be able to do it simply by *instructions* (eg, you must complete this in one hour) provided you have correctly calculated the level and amount to be done; or you may use certain presentation media to help ensure it. It is easier to control pace with an 'ephemeral' medium so that the student has to keep up. The difficulty lies in ensuring that everyone is satisfied.

In practice the problem is often twofold.

(i) You may have a set period of time to cover in which case you have to decide whether to aim at the average, provide extra for fast workers and help the slow, or . . .

(ii) you may have a set amount of work to cover in which case you need to consider the slow workers and provide extra (enrichment? extension?) for various degrees of faster progress.

You might find it useful, when you have a problem of control to go back to exercise . . . on p 40 and apply it.

(3) *Recording of results*

You may, just as in teaching, want the student to have a permanent record of what he has done — and the more you use external resources (ie, not in his possession) the more of a problem this becomes. You can:

(i) incorporate the record in the student work material — by completing blanks, filling in diagrams, etc. An advantage is that you can ensure he ends up with properly organised summaries, good diagrams, etc, which will form a useful aide mémoire.

On the other hand the material is then not re-usable, and you can really use this only for formats (3) and (4) with all that that implies.

(ii) Prepare special summaries for the student to file after completion of the task. It has the same advantages as that above but it can really only be used where you know the results beforehand (closed-ended); he may come to rely on them instead of doing the work.

(iii) Arrange, via instructions and suggestions, for the student to compile his own 'record' — either with external aids (eg, provision of blank diagrams) or without. It is more personal to the student but you need to identify what is to be recorded and to what standard. It can involve much time-consuming copying and requires careful design of the student materials and organisation of the work.

(iv) Accept what the student produces as the 'record'. Advantages are that you are relieved of work and that the student is not constrained. You have to give specific guidance if you want a particular standard. The more mature and advanced the pupil, the better it works.

There may of course be many times when you don't feel the student needs a record or you are unconcerned about the standard (eg, when he is in the early stages of developing learning skills). In that case (iv) is useful since it can become a diagnostic device!

(4) *The fourth principle is that of 'response-structuring'*, a technical but descriptive term which simply substitutes for the guidance and interpretation element in teaching.

If a teacher wishes to ensure that a point is taken, or is confronted by a misunderstanding, he can take action on the spot. Once again you have to identify such problems beforehand and build solutions into your material. The student is likely to be engaged on active learning and therefore will be responding to problems, suggestions, etc, built into the material or assignment task. You might like to pause and jot down various ways in which you can use the material structure to elicit responses from your students.

Well that is one of them: ask a question and then provide answers. You could:

   (i)   ask questions which leave a certain amount of freedom and then give suggested answers for a student to match *his* answers against

  (ii)   ask questions requiring specific right answers and then confirm them

 (iii)   ask questions giving a choice of answers and discuss the results

 (iv)   refer the student to information, etc, which will solve any queries

  (v)   set the student a task and then review the results.

In all of these there is the principle of *response* by student (to stimulus) leading to what is called *feedback* (information about his response) which in turn may

— confirm his response
— diagnose a problem and guide him to remediation
— spell out possible choices of 'route' he can take.

The important things to be able to decide are:

WHEN— how frequently do you feel the student needs to be made to respond and to be given information?

WHY— in what circumstances is it needed: is the task one that is self-fulfilling? how mature is the student?

HOW— what types of responses are appropriate to the learning being undertaken?

It is also important to note that 'response structuring' does not necessarily mean very small pieces of learning. The only explicit response of a student may be successful completion of the assignment. On the other hand he may, in a practice situation for example, be making a response every time he completes a practice item.

    Two general rules apply:

   (i)   any response you want to feed back information on must be useful — too often we ask trivial or irrelevant questions which do not help to mediate the learning for the student

(ii)   the more circumscribed and closed-ended the work is, the more useful feedback becomes as a mediating tool and the more frequently you need to make the student respond to specific stimuli.

This is not always easy to judge: for example, I am judging that you are capable of considering a lot of information here with very little feedback to yourself in the way of checks; if I am wrong you will be feeling slightly overwhelmed — and that is how *your* student may feel if you feed him too much information without helping him to assimilate it.

So much for principles: let us now look at some of the ways in which we can structure the student material in detail. These apply both to the production of 'new' material and to the modification of existing information resources. Those considered are the problems of designing

— instructions (p 157)
— procedures (p 159)
— questions (p 160)
— step-by-step learning (p 163)
— feedback (p 164)

The discussion is deliberately *not* confined to any one particular medium (eg, a paper worksheet) since the ideas discussed can be used to produce material in any appropriate medium.

Usefulness of these ideas really depends on what function(s) you want the material to undertake.

(a)   'Direct'— to tell a student where to go and what to do; to take a student through a task
(b)   'Guide'— to help a student work out a problem; to suggest ways of tackling a task
(c)   'Teach'— to inculcate knowledge, etc, by actually teaching the student to facilitate the learning so that most of the advances are made by the student but a set goal is achievable.

Giving directions or instruction(s)
(1)   Remember *you* are not there so any directions or

instructions must be clear and explicit: eg, 'go and find out . . . ', even if the student has the learning skills, is acceptable only if he is aware of the place he will find the information; already knows how to get there; can locate — or get help in locating — the exact source.

(2)   Use diagrams or other aids if words alone might be ambiguous: eg, 'Set up the apparatus by fixing an XYZ cup in its stand the right way up', is not so clear as:

1. Put the XYZ cup on its stand.

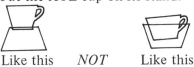

Like this   *NOT*   Like this

(3)   If the student will need to keep referring to the directions, put them in a physical form he can take with him. (If you think that is obvious it is not: the number of media-fixated packages which use, say, a fixed tape recorder to instruct a student to 'go and get . . . ', 'now go to X and . . . ' is legion.)
PRESENTATION CHARACTERISTICS SHOULD FIT THE FORMAT.

(4)   Check if any *feedback* will be needed by the student to show him he has carried out the directions and make sure it is there: (eg, (i) in finding a book, the *title* will tell him, so you may not need any more (ii) in example (2) above, the diagram can be compared with the real apparatus). If in doubt you could amplify it.
Directions are only viable if you can both be confident they will work.

small ⟶ ring upwards

(5)   If in doubt provide an emergency let-out: (eg, 'if you can't find it, see your teacher', 'ask your teacher to check your completed apparatus').

Instructions can only be simple directions if you are sure they are sufficient. You may introduce guidance elements, as in the diagrams, but if you do it is likely they are really needed. You should also look at p 164 on feedback.

Procedures

Procedures are basically guidelines intended to enable a user to follow a process or go along a route and, so far as we are concerned, are of two kinds. They are useful where *decision making* is the important element in the work.

(1) 'Search procedures' are where you use the guide to find an answer to one or more problems but without learning the process in so doing. It simply enables you to achieve the desired result. An example of a search procedure known as an algorithm is shown on p 165 – it depends on being able to formulate precise questions in a worked-out order.

    You arrived here from p 157 by means of a simple, though disguised search procedure. As another example, an index with location references is the basis of a search procedure. Search procedures are useful where you want a student to investigate the implications of various courses of action and to be able to identify the consequences; and where you want to guide him to certain items.

(2) *Learning procedures* are useful where you want to teach a student to undertake a particular task (say, to learn a computational skill) – the application of rules to examples, or the identification of general rules from a variety of relevant and irrelevant examples.

    If it is very frequently used, a search procedure can also be a learning procedure in that you can finally do without it – you have learnt how to get the answers. There is no intrinsic difference from search procedures, it is simply the method of use – in 'learning' from it you arrange the material so that the student uses it again and again until he is familiar with the ways of reaching the answer.

    Hopefully, if you use it, the radial diagram on p 176 becomes a learning procedure. You can therefore use the method (however you present it) to develop learning skills (eg, how to extract information) by applying the same procedure to chosen information stimulus materials, or as a guide simply to enable students to get to a particular piece of information or to one item among a number of others.

There is no short cut but the information index on p 195 may give you some guidance as to further reading. A procedure can be:

(a)   a set of clear instructions
(b)   a checklist – which alerts you to the need for decision
(c)   a decision-making instrument to achieve an end
(d)   a tool for learning or guiding through a process to develop learning or content skills.

Questioning

A great deal of work has been done on basic modes of questioning and their purposes and it would be foolish to try to reinvent the wheel here; this section therefore owes much to the many people who have worked on the problems of comprehension. It is often argued that questions can in general be divided into four categories which might be called:

(1)   *Cognitive memory:* ie, recall of facts or other items already learnt (eg, 'What is the largest city in Europe?'). The answer is known or it is not.

(2)   *Convergent:* the analysis and integration of data – which can ask for reasoning or just for recall of a number of associated items (eg, 'What is there about the position of London that accounts for its importance?').

(3)   *Divergent:* the application of acquired data to new situations in an imaginative and creative way (eg, 'How might the lives of the people of London be different if the city were located in a torrid zone?').

(4)   *Evaluative:* the consideration of value judgement and choice – either broad requiring a reasoned evaluation or narrow (eg, requiring a simple yes or no).

The categories generally match up with the ideas of convergent and divergent thinking.

The problem with using those categories as they stand is

that they assume that the person questioned is to answer from his own experience. We on the other hand are designing material which cannot make that assumption: indeed it may need specifically to be facilitating the acquisition of new data and experience for the student so that we need to look at questions from a slightly different viewpoint. 'What is the largest city in Europe?' for example is only viable if

(i)   we can assume the student already has the information – in which case in terms of individualised learning it is no more than a test question; or

(ii) we want the student to find out the data and have provided a guide (plus information resources) for him to use.

Questions to facilitate extraction and comprehension of data
Firstly we should note that, if we are to avoid pure 'rote extraction' it is necessary to ask selected questions on at least three levels and possibly four:

(1)   you need to ask questions about the overall theme(s) of the information – to find out if the student understands what he is trying to do

(2)   you need to ask questions about any details you have identified as important, to ensure that the student has picked them up, too

(3)   you need, where possible, to ask him to draw one or more conclusions from what he has extracted – to check that he is actually analysing and integrating the data. This is particularly important.

(4)   If there are any vital keywords – specialised vocabulary or concept descriptions – you should ask questions to check if the student has assimilated their meaning in the context.

Having said that, you can see that your questions may, even there, involve all four categories, but with problems because you are not just asking for recall to start with.

(i)   They can be phrased as simple 'cognitive memory' questions only if we treat the information container as a 'memory' rather like a computer memory — but that needs instructions to enable people to get at it. Therefore any such questions must be linked to instructions or guidance as to how to find the information.

(ii) Unlike direct questioning you need to consider how to provide feedback which the student can use to judge his own progress (see p 164).

Questions to facilitate application and evaluation of data
The main problem here is to determine whether you want a convergent approach, which you can use to control the learning or a divergent one which is much more open-ended. Furthermore, once again, you cannot justifiably ask such questions unless —

(1) you are sure that the student already has the capacity (in knowledge and experience) to answer them usefully to himself or

(2) you have preceded them with work and questioning involving the extraction, consideration and integration of any relevant data.

In producing student work schemes and material there is a definite questioning hierarchy, especially if your material is not to be open-ended. To be sure of asking the right question you need to

(i) know why you are asking it
(ii) be able yourself to identify the right answer or answers
(iii) identify the appropriate feedback, which is dependent on (i) and (ii)
(iv) be sure either that the question is the result of guidance which will enable the student to find the answer, or that the student has the capability to answer without any help.

Step-by-step learning

Where you want the student to carry out specified processes involving thought or operation, an extension of procedural work is to split the information or tasks you want him to learn into 'bite-sized pieces', pass on to him as much as you think he can assimilate in one gulp and then ask him to make a response so that he can:

— check for himself if he has understood/carried out the work

— see what the effects of any element of choice may be.

This technique has always been the basis of frame writing in the programmed learning technique and is certainly most effective when that technique is used because it defines the objectives, and hence the responses needed, and analyses out the information or stimulus content. The frame writing idea, however, can be used on its own provided you are fairly certain of getting the right level, you know what you want to do, you can ask the right questions and provide relevant feedback. Its main problem is a tendency to ask for irrelevant responses: often characterised by what PL people used to call 'filling in the holes in the cheese'. In other words a technique whereby students fill in missing words to complete a statement. 'What do you think is the problem of   in holes in the   ? (fill in the missing words).

Well that is the problem isn't it? If you filled in those words they would not advance your learning in any way, yet many work materials sprinkle gaps around quite arbitrarily in the fond belief that their completion assists learning.

If you are going to use this technique the responses you are asked to make must be relevant, you need to guard against making your questions too open ended and the level of 'bite' must be right — too big and the student may not comprehend, too small and he soon finds it easy and gets bored.

In Appendix 3 there is a short step-by-step sequence on 'thinking aloud diagrams' which appears to work but certainly shows two of those problems. Can you identify them and also identify a way in which it tries to remedy any difficulty caused by them?

The problems are whether the 'bite size' is right in the context of possibly unfamiliar subject matter; and whether the questions are specific enough. The way it tries to remedy them is by use of immediate feedback on what was intended, so that the reader can come back to argument if he has wandered off track. If you would like to go further into this subject look in the information index under 'sequencing of instruction'.

Ways of providing feedback

The idea of feedback is generally applicable to any material writing technique that requires the student to know how he is getting on.

(1) Feedback to the student

For *questions* you can
– simply give the answer where it is likely to be right
– give the answer and an explanation in case of misunderstanding
– frame the question to give an unambiguous answer (eg, 'yes' or 'no') and use this to guide the student
– provide alternative answers and use them to diagnose and correct errors or misunderstandings.

(To give useful feedback you must be able to identify *why* you are using that particular question at that particular time.)

For *learning tasks*
– provide model answers
– identify crucial points and provide a check for the student, so that he can obtain help if he is going wrong.

For *procedures*
– structure questions to make results of a decision determine the next step
– provide guidance in a different form from the instruction (eg, a diagram to cross-check a written direction).

(2) Feedback to the teacher/manager

The best means of obtaining feedback in student work material is to build yourself in at crucial points so that the student is instructed to come and bring his work to you. You will need to identify the crucial points!

Procedure for selecting formats and media
This procedure assumes that you have defined the goals and purposes of your assignment, and that you have identified the function or functions you want the *student work material* to perform. Now you need an appropriate way of presenting it to the student.

Work through the procedure (the algorithm which begins overleaf) by answering the questions and following the appropriate arrows.

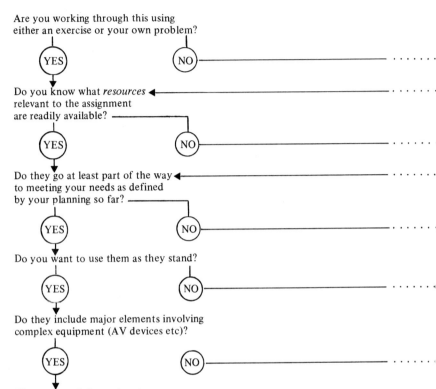

Are you working through this using
either an exercise or your own problem?

YES   **NO** ———————————————————— · · · · · ·

Do you know what *resources* ◄———————————————————— · · · · · · ·
relevant to the assignment
are readily available? ————————┐

YES   **NO** ———————————————————— · · · · · ·

Do they go at least part of the way ◄———————————————— · · · · · · ·
to meeting your needs as defined
by your planning so far? ————————┐

YES   **NO** ———————————————————— · · · · · ·

Do you want to use them as they stand?

YES   **NO** ———————————————————— · · · · · ◄

Do they include major elements involving
complex equipment (AV devices etc)?

YES   **NO** ———————————————————— · · · · · ·

They may well determine the
overall medium and hence
the format. Turn to page 170.

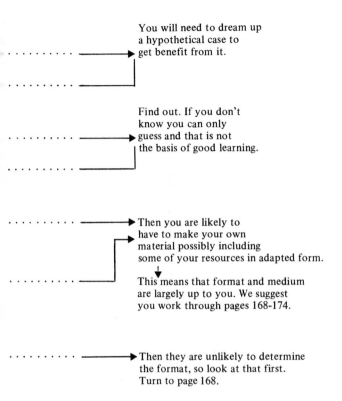

· · · · · · · · · ·   You will need to dream up
a hypothetical case to
get benefit from it.

· · · · · · · ·

· · · · · · · · · ·   Find out. If you don't
know you can only
guess and that is not
the basis of good learning.

· · · · · · · ·

· · · · · · · · · ·   Then you are likely to
have to make your own
material possibly including
some of your resources in adapted form.

· · · · · · · · · ·   This means that format and medium
are largely up to you. We suggest
you work through pages 168-174.

· · · · · · · · · ·   Then they are unlikely to determine
the format, so look at that first.
Turn to page 168.

Choosing a format (refer to p 143 for details of formats)

	Possible reasons	
(1)	They need to be used by a whole group at once.	Do you need to produce your own materials? ——————— · · · · · ·
	No appropriate resource items are available.	(NO)
(2)	Needs complex equipment.	Are there any media constraints imposed by the resource items? ——————— · · · · · ·
		(NO)
(3)	They are held in the library as reference items. They are part of the environment.	Do the *resource items* require student to move about? ——————— · · · · · ·
		(NO)
(4)	The activities involve movement (eg, measuring a number of scattered items)	Does the learning task require the student to move about? ——————— · · · · · ·
		(NO)
(5)	Because of level, or because the student does not have necessary learning skills.	Do the resource items need interpreting? ——————— · · · · · ·
		(NO)
(6)	You may be uncertain in which case play safe.	Are you *sure* the student has the necessary learning and content skills? ——————— · · · · · ·
		(NO)
		Use format 2. ——————— · · · · · ·

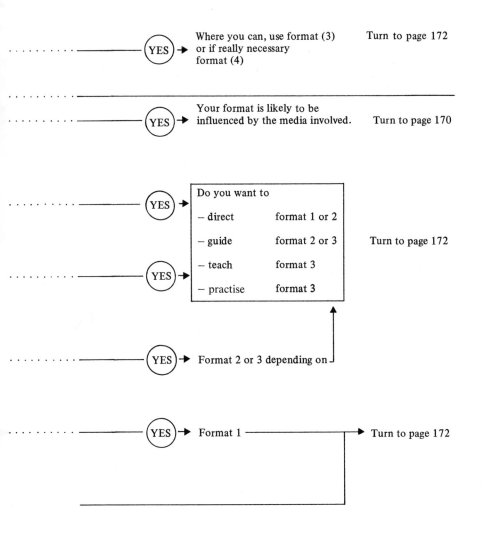

Where you can, use format (3)   Turn to page 172
or if really necessary
format (4)

Your format is likely to be
influenced by the media involved.   Turn to page 170

Do you want to

– direct   format 1 or 2

– guide   format 2 or 3

– teach   format 3

– practise   format 3

Turn to page 172

Format 2 or 3 depending on

Format 1

Turn to page 172

Planning student material involving existing resources

Possible reasons

Film, TV, synchronised tape/slide? This may mean they have to.	Do the chosen resources involve the use of complex or not easily portable ———————— · · · · · · ◀ equipment?
	(NO)
— the instructions are part of the teaching as in a learning program. — the stimulus may have instructions physically marked on it.	Do they contain instructions integrated with any stimulus material? ——————— · · · · · · (NO)
Could be a set of 'directions'.	Do they contain instructions only? ——————— · · · · · · (NO)
It could include a set of slides and a separate tape or a tape and a piece of paper or a book.	Almost certainly they are stimulus material. Your format and medium for the *instruction* element is your own choice. Is the *stimulus* material element both audio and ——————— · · · · · · visual? (NO)
eg, a set of slides, a chart, a model	Has it visual elements only? ——————— · · · · · · (NO)
eg, an audio tape to listen to	Is it audio only? ——————— · · · · · · (NO)
Work on texture or smell where this is important.	It must be connected with smell or touch. Neither impose serious format limitations.

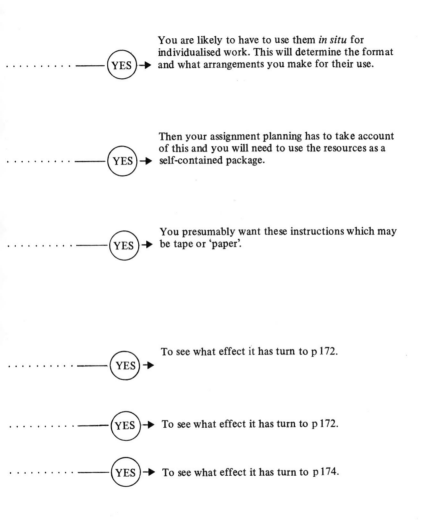

YES → You are likely to have to use them *in situ* for individualised work. This will determine the format and what arrangements you make for their use.

YES → Then your assignment planning has to take account of this and you will need to use the resources as a self-contained package.

YES → You presumably want these instructions which may be tape or 'paper'.

YES → To see what effect it has turn to p 172.

YES → To see what effect it has turn to p 172.

YES → To see what effect it has turn to p 174.

Choosing a medium appropriate to the task – 1

Possible reasons

– a scientific experiment
– a mathematical operation
– a task in the local
  environment
	Is the task a practical one? — — — — — · · · · · ·
	  │
	  (NO)
	  ↓

– need to show moving
  scenes not otherwise
  available
– need simply to show
  movement to explain a
  point
	Will you need moving — — — — — · · · · · ·
	  visuals?
	  │
	  (NO)
	  ↓

– need to reproduce
  paintings, photos,
  views of real scenes
  (eg, the local farm)
	Will you need still pictures
	  requiring high definition — — — — · · · · · ·
	  and quality (accuracy of
	  colour, etc)?
	  │
	  (NO)
	  ↓

	Will you need patterns, — — — — — · · · · · ·
	  diagrams or line symbols?
	  │
	  (NO)
	  ↓

– need to acquire
  appreciation of shape
  as a property
	Will you need the student — — — — — · · · · · ·
	  to handle the stimulus?
	  │
	  (NO)
	  ↓

Identification of
particular smells related
to learning taking place.
	Does smell play a part? — — — — — · · · · · ·
	  │
	  (NO)
	  ↓

Specific sounds are
essential as part of the
work.
Student cannot read at
appropriate level of skill.
Student motivated by voice.
	Will you need to use sound — — — — · · · · · ·
	  as well as visuals?
	  │
	  (NO)
	  ↓ Turn to p 175.

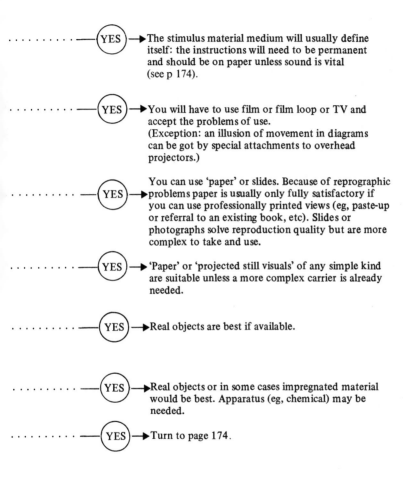

· · · · · · · · · · — (YES) → The stimulus material medium will usually define itself: the instructions will need to be permanent and should be on paper unless sound is vital (see p 174).

· · · · · · · · · · — (YES) → You will have to use film or film loop or TV and accept the problems of use.
(Exception: an illusion of movement in diagrams can be got by special attachments to overhead projectors.)

· · · · · · · · · · — (YES) → You can use 'paper' or slides. Because of reprographic problems paper is usually only fully satisfactory if you can use professionally printed views (eg, paste-up or referral to an existing book, etc). Slides or photographs solve reproduction quality but are more complex to take and use.

· · · · · · · · · · — (YES) → 'Paper' or 'projected still visuals' of any simple kind are suitable unless a more complex carrier is already needed.

· · · · · · · · · · — (YES) → Real objects are best if available.

· · · · · · · · · · — (YES) → Real objects or in some cases impregnated material would be best. Apparatus (eg, chemical) may be needed.

· · · · · · · · · · — (YES) → Turn to page 174.

Choosing a medium appropriate to the task −2

Possible reasons	
You want student to interview someone. To listen to something going on at a particular moment.	You need *sound.* Do you intend to use live ————— · · · · · · sound?
	↓ (NO)
To lessen the 'ephemeral' effect.	You will be using recorded sound. Does it need to be ————— · · · · · · easily replayable?
	↓ (NO)
On a gramophone record − someone has already recorded it.	Is it in an already available form? ————— · · · · · ◄
	↓ (NO)
You wish to control the pace of the student. You feel it is vital that the sound and visual elements match.	Does it *need* to be physically linked with a visual element? ————— · · · · · ◄
	↓ (NO)
You want to let the student control his own pace but still want matching.	Is it desirable that sound and vision are linked? ————— · · · · · ◄
	↓ (NO)
	Use the simplest form you can so long as other learning factors allow (typically tape and 'paper'). Turn to p 176.

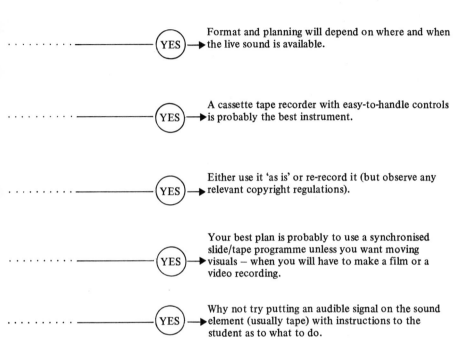

· · · · · · · · · · ———————— (YES)→ Format and planning will depend on where and when
the live sound is available.

· · · · · · · · · ———————— (YES)→ A cassette tape recorder with easy-to-handle controls
is probably the best instrument.

· · · · · · · · · ———————— (YES)→ Either use it 'as is' or re-record it (but observe any
relevant copyright regulations).

· · · · · · · · · ———————— (YES)→ Your best plan is probably to use a synchronised
slide/tape programme unless you want moving
visuals – when you will have to make a film or a
video recording.

· · · · · · · · ———————— (YES)→ Why not try putting an audible signal on the sound
element (usually tape) with instructions to the
student as to what to do.

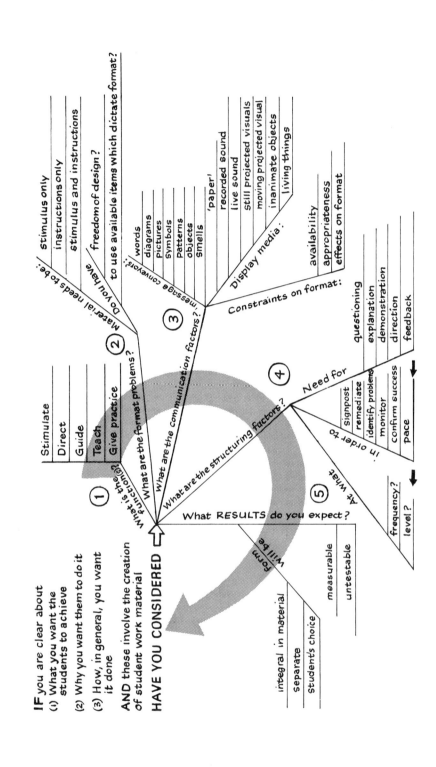

IF you are clear about
(1) What you want the students to achieve
(2) Why you want them to do it
(3) How, in general, you want it done

AND these involve the creation of student work material

HAVE YOU CONSIDERED

① What is the function(s)?

Stimulate
Direct
Guide
Teach
Give practice

② What are the format problems?

Material needs to be:
stimulus only
instructions only
stimulus and instructions

Do you have
freedom of design?
to use available items which dictate format?

③ What are the communication factors?

message conveyors:
words
diagrams
pictures
Symbols
Patterns
objects
smells

Display media:
'paper'
recorded sound
live sound
still projected visuals
moving projected visual
inanimate objects
living things

Constraints on format:
availability
appropriateness
effects on format

④ What are the structuring factors?

Need for
questioning
explanation
demonstration
direction
feedback

in order to
signpost
remediate
identify problems
monitor
confirm success
pace

⑤ What RESULTS do you expect?

At what
frequency?
level?

Form will be
integral in material
separate
Student's choice
measurable
untestable

9. Putting it all together

All the discussion and advice so far in this book has been about discrete elements of the teaching/learning process — and particularly about elements which differ from those of traditional group teaching. It thus risks two possible failures.

(1) The first danger is under-emphasising the fact that 'individualised' and 'resource-oriented' techniques are not sufficient in themselves. They must be regarded as only part of a much bigger whole that may consist largely of traditional teaching situations. Thus they need to fit into an overall framework *and* they need a great deal of effort to use successfully.

So, if you decide to use such techniques at any time, ought you not seriously to ask yourself:

(i) Exactly *what* area of the work are you going to cover by these methods and *why*
 — because there seem to be a lot of useful outside resources?
 — because the group structure makes formal teaching difficult?
 — because you want to experiment?

(ii) What good reasons are there for supposing that your decision will improve the students' learning? How does what you are planning differ from your normal teaching and how is it better than that? (and what are its *dis*advantages?)

(iii) How is anything you do likely to interact or conflict with the learning/teaching strategies of colleagues? Are the students going to have lesson after lesson using worksheets on a variety of subjects, or will they get variations in type of work because of the ideas of different teachers?

(2) The second danger is that it may reinforce a tendency to separate the innovative teacher's functions into 'management of resources' and 'management of learning', a danger that is not alleviated by the fact that special interests among innovators tend to make us each concentrate on one aspect.

You might like at this point to think of another way of sorting out the functions of a teacher-manager?

Perhaps we could better be thinking of

organisation ⎫
implementation ⎬   of resources and learning in parallel?
evaluation ⎭

What we are doing after all is a continual process and if the parts of that process do not interact on each other then it may break down. The table opposite represents the process.

Of the three parts, *organisation*, both of the learning and the resources needed to support it, has been covered in some detail. The essential element is that it involves mainly advance preparation to ensure that learning takes place in as advantageous conditions as possible.

Implementation is more difficult: you can plan for and organise a particular pattern of work but you need also to be certain *why* you want that pattern and what it actually involves you and the students in doing. Let us start from the concept of group teaching since it is a desire to break away from that which motivates many of us towards individualising work.

Group teaching implies that at any one time the same subject matter, skills, etc, are being taught, usually at one level of difficulty, to a fairly homogeneous collection of students. The most frequent reasons for 'changing', other than a desire to experiment, are that the ability range of the group is becoming very wide or that you feel your students, if simply exposed to learning experiences, may learn better than you can teach them. The results range from a virtual transfer of teaching on to work sheets, to a belief that if the student is allowed free rein he will be able to decide what to learn and then be able to learn it because he is motivated to do so.

Process for teacher managing learning

Organisation	*Comments*
1.1 Establishes purpose, type and content of course	NB, more often an on-going situation than a new formulation.
1.2 Establishes student characteristics	As above.
1.3 Establishes learning criteria	
1.4 Identifies resource/ constraint factors	
1.5 Identifies most viable teaching/learning methods	
1.6 Uses above factors to plan the work	Design
Implements	
2.1 Physically organises available resources	
2.2 Produces necessary items	
2.3 Teaches and/or guides student learning	Aids and materials depending on chosen methods.
2.4 Monitors student activities	
2.5 Assesses success of the learning	
Evaluates	
3.1 Uses results of 2.4; 2.5 to define any problems	
3.2 Establishes from 3.1 the need for, types and problems of implementing any modifications	NB, actual modification is another cycle of the process.
Validates	
4.1 Uses information from 2.4; 2.5; 3.2 to help bring his courses and/or materials to a predetermined standard.	

If you are a believer in 'free discovery' at all costs then this book cannot help you; it presupposes the need for structure to facilitate learning. At the other end of the scale, we tend perhaps to over-structure, to get fixated by one approach just as one can get obsessed by one medium to the exclusion of all else. A 'learning country analogy' might be that we constantly take the student over almost identical routes, sometimes by inappropriate means, while believing he is seeing all the country that exists.

Even so far as genuinely individualised learning is concerned this would be a dubious process. In that many of us tend to drift into it from a perceived need to *teach a subject* at different levels rather than to *help different students learn* about a subject it can be actively discouraging.

Take, for example, the most common form of 'individualised work' at secondary-school level, where the content of teaching has simply been written down on worksheets and the entire group progresses through these towards a common goal. It is not an easy option, usually involving a massive amount of work by the teachers concerned, and we claim correspondingly big advantages for it: specific ones are that our work is better prepared and that we can make different levels of work for students of differing ability. At the same time we need to recognise that the approach has corresponding disadvantages: it is less flexible than teaching; it is more timetable-sensitive because of variations in student work-speed; we tend, owing to outside pressures, to 'get in a rut' and produce repetitive, similar worksheets which may not be appropriate for all tasks. Even if we have identified group work materials as appropriate, to use them successfully, we still have to overcome these problems.

Students putting away half-done work at the end of a lesson period; students grumbling about 'yet another worksheet'; a constant flow of student queries on trivial points: all these point to unsatisfactory design and management of the learning process.

In the same way, just turning a student loose on to a bank of resource materials is likely to produce an almost unmanageable situation which counter-balances any advantages it may have. Unless you have the means of organising, controlling and monitoring what is going on it is really an abrogation of your responsibility.

Having said that it is, fortunately, true that guidelines can go only so far. The teacher, given tools, is still the only person who has the knowledge and skills in particular situations to judge what to do and how to do it – or to ensure that it is done. The details of management are yours alone *but* management rather than pure administration is essential.

Are you preoccupied with
– rushing round answering trivial queries
– marking things students could check themselves
– administering the distribution and collection of work cards, etc?

Are you unaware of
– what most students are doing at any one time
– what problems are likely to arise and where the answers may be found
– the constraints within which you are working (so you can manipulate them)?

If so, then we suggest you are not really *managing* the work; you are letting the situation run you and that is the wrong way round.

And if you are not involved not only in organising and implementing but also in evaluation, then one of your main management tools is missing. Even if you plan carefully, you need to evaluate. The more you incline to the 'post-evaluated' point of view the more you are going to need evaluative procedures, but evaluation itself is not simple. What do you think to be the main purposes of evaluating a piece of individual learning from your viewpoint?

For you as teacher/manager its purposes are probably:

(i) to find out whether what your students have done was worthwhile

(ii) if it was worthwhile, to establish whether they learnt effectively (successfully and with adequate motivation in the time you were able to allow them); to find out if it could have been more effective and, if so, how

(iii) if it was not worthwhile, to discover what you should do instead.

To establish these findings you have available three major types of evaluative procedures which are often called formative, summative and illuminative evaluation.

To put it simply (perhaps over-simply) . . .

Formative evaluation is an extension of the monitoring process in which you use indications from the work in progress actually to help you alter it while it is going on. You are in fact changing the learning process as it happens.

Summative evaluation is what most of us do. It involves assessing the success of learning once it is completed and judging the results of tests, or other assessment procedures. You can then use the results to modify future work.

Illuminative evaluation is much less clearly defined but means roughly what it says: you use monitoring of a learning situation to discover what is happening and then judge whether what you find is worthwhile according to internal criteria — student satisfaction, your own impressions, what goals you can 'extract' from the learning activities being undertaken. Its ethos says, essentially, that in many cases you cannot plan a course of learning thoroughly — or that, if you do, the reality is quite likely to differ widely from your original concept.

All these have their uses but their overall problem is that the stricter you make your actual procedures (the more you tend towards formal techniques of summative evaluation) the more narrowly you are judging the success of the learning; it is often argued that you may well thereby restrict the learning undertaken. The wider you make your evaluative techniques the less possible it is to define the problems of specific learning assignments and activities.

In practice, given time and other constraints, you as the teacher/manager really have only four ways of evaluating what your students are doing.

(i)   Setting tests and other formal assessment devices
(ii) Monitoring formally and recording progress

These two assume pre-organised work.

(iii) Observing and drawing conclusions
(iv) Obtaining impressions from the students

These two can help to evaluate either type of work.

We would suggest that, although you may initially believe in not organising the work closely in advance, any form of evaluation is likely to lead you to organising in advance for future patterns of work, because that is implicit in the judgements of what constitutes 'worthwhile' and 'need for modification'. It may also lead you to modify what is going on and in doing so you are beginning to organise once again. We would suggest that: 'Ah well, but I didn't really mean that' is usually the precursor of a little formative evaluation in progress. 'Please Miss, what are we supposed to be doing?' may well be illuminating and once again lead both to definition and modification of work either organised in advance or entered upon on the spur of the moment.

In either case a problem has been identified but what the problems and what the answers may be can only be found by examining your own organisation and preparation of the work. If you want to know more about evaluation we suggest you look in the information index on p 195.

So, managing a situation, we suggest, involves organisation, implementation and evaluation. If the activities defined by all three processes do not link up — if, even worse, they conflict — then the learning is unlikely to be successful. If they do link up and you can use the various 'tools' to provide suitable activities and materials for your students then you have a good chance of succeeding.

If you want to explore the three elements further, a short self-contained discussion exercise follows.

Exercise on managing learning
Introduction
This exercise is intended to allow you to explore possible

ways in which you as a teacher can manage a learning situation so as to control or influence the student work that is taking place. It consists of an 'aide-mémoire' which sums up what we have already been talking about, a series of problems for you to study, and a matrix of possible management actions you can apply to help solve those problems. When you have selected the actions you think are most suitable you can turn to a page where the implications of your selection will be discussed. In itself the process also provides an example of one way in which you can produce individualised discussion material.

Information
Please read this before tackling the problems on p186. At various points in this book we have discussed briefly the problems of controlling various patterns of teaching and learning (ie, being able at will to influence them). We concluded that only where the control dimension was fairly strong was it possible to organise resource-based work which had readily identifiable and achievable goals. Thus, of the two possible main approaches.

– the post-evaluative one by its very nature can only be managed by observing what is going on and then deducing how it can be influenced
– the pre-organised one is susceptible to being managed because of the opportunities it offers but often the most useful control elements are not used.

The only element common to both approaches – and a common element in all attempts to influence students' active learning – is feedback, the constant interchange of information either directly or indirectly between teacher/manager and student. Assuming that 'control' = ability to influence or manage learning, however, the effectiveness of the feedback must depend on the effectiveness of other elements in a learning situation. It is no good providing for constant teacher/student communication if neither of you knows what the other is talking about or if you cannot readily provide answers to a student's queries.

Such factors are not implicit in learning. To exercise any desired amount and quality of management over a given learning situation, external factors must be brought into play by teacher-manager or student and these may be applied to the organisation, implementation or evaluation aspects as shown overleaf.
They are:

A. Clarification of the original aim — to what extent one can define the learning goals so that it is possible to determine exactly what the student is expected to achieve as a minimum end product of his work.

B. Detailed analysis of the learning involved in achieving A — note that this does not imply dictating *how* it is to be learnt but is a map of the learning country. It shows what difficulties may be encountered, and where various routes and approaches may lead. It may also show clearly what existing knowledge the student may be expected to have and what content is to be covered.

C. Structuring of the environment — this can be done in varying degrees of subtlety to reduce the choice of actions and select the resources available to the student and thus minimise monitoring and distraction problems; (eg, if learning to use a simple balance, he may be provided with pre-weighed objects instead of using anything lying around. This enables quick feedback in case of difficulty).

D. Structuring of the learning assignments or material — if desired, learning assignments and materials can be so organised that by working through them a given student will, by the end of the work, be able to achieve a clearly defined learning goal . . . or they can be designed to exert any desired degree of control over the learning. The problem is that the more controlled they are, the less flexible they become.

E. Monitoring of the learning process — using the student's work and his reactions as a diagnostic aid to help you guide him. This is the main vehicle for feedback.

F. Evaluating the learning — using the results of the students'

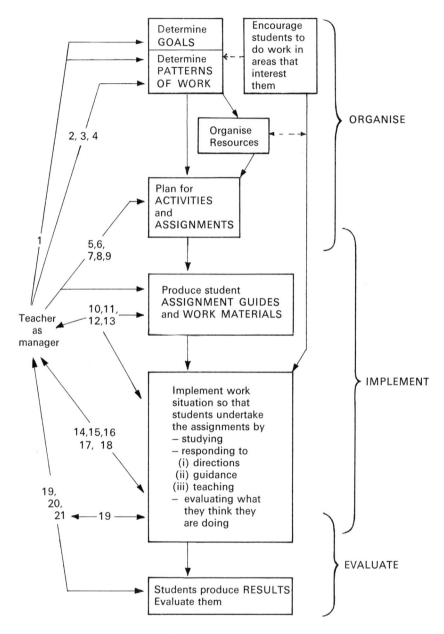

Management influences on individualised learning. Numbers refer to the matrix of management tasks on p 188.

work together with information from $A-E$, in order to assess how well learning has taken place and whether any aspects need modifying.

Note that all the comments above refer mainly to managing the work of individual students. As the number of students increases, the control possible by means of monitoring and evaluation alone decreases. Why? Because the time available rarely increases in proportion, you can usually monitor a group's progress only by spot-checks; it is even more difficult if the 'group' is composed of students working individually on different assignments. These limitations mean that with one teacher and a large number of students, organisation activities become vital if any serious management is to take place.

Exercise: selecting appropriate management tools. Below you will find a series of problems related to a matrix of statements about management activities. Please follow the instructions and you will involve yourself in a short discussion about how to manage the situations described.

For each of these problems in turn:

(1)   Look at the diagram and the matrix.

(2)   Select the management tools you think would be appropriate to allow you to manage the learning, noting them under the three broad areas of:
      (i) organisation − those you would use in planning
      (ii) implementation − those you would use in guiding and assessing the work in progress
      (iii) evaluation − those you would use to judge how well your learning plans, etc, have enabled the student to succeed.

(3)   Turn to the page indicated and read the discussion.

1 Provide, or agree in advance, minimum learning goals.	**2** Map the 'learning country' in advance to identify problems, possible routes, etc.	**3** Define clearly the student(s) existing knowledge, skills, etc, relevant to the learning you want undertaken.
4 Define clearly what *content* (subject matter) the student is actually going to learn or be taught.	**5** Decide to structure the environment to guide student choice.	**6** Decide to structure assignments and materials to ensure success so far as possible (eg, step-by-step learning).
7 Set a time limit by which students should complete the learning tasks.	**8** Plan ahead to take advantage of any useful side-track or new approach from the student.	**9** Have clear knowledge of possible lines of discovery and where they lead to.
10 Provide different assignments and/or materials to suit *each* individual student.	**11** Provide parallel work materials at differing levels of difficulty.	**12** Build in (to materials etc) feedback to student at points of difficulty, etc.
13 Build in feedback for teacher about student(s)'progress (eg, by referrals).	**14** Monitor progress of all students periodically by spot-checks.	**15** Guide progress of student by tutorial sessions at intervals.
16 Require student to check his own progress and be responsible for coming to teacher if in doubt.	**17** Require students to record their own progress in terms of work done.	**18** Keep detailed records of progress for each student.
19 Provide assessment at intervals by formal testing.	**20** Formally test achievement of learning goals on completion of work.	**21** Use completed work/ assignment results as means of assessment.

Problem 1
A student is to carry out an individual project involving a search for information, carrying out a small 'experiment' and writing up his results — the subject is to be agreed between teacher and student. (p190).

Problem 2
A group of students, working individually, are to carry out related work on a 'class' project involving searches for information, using that information and collaborating to produce an exhibition of work as the communal result. (p191).

Problem 3
A student is to carry out some individual work on a subject of his own choice (possibly within an overall range of possibilities: would this make any difference?). (p192).

Problem 4
You intend to make a 'contract' with a student whereby he will make himself responsible for doing the agreed work under the conditions you agree with him. The work will last for several weeks. (p193).

Problem 5
You wish to teach some skills to a group of students by using a structured work scheme, which they can work through individually. You expect the scheme to take account of differences in ability, etc. (p194).

Problem 1 — A student doing an individual project you want to influence but not dictate to
You can influence the work at all stages but some actions are likely to be easier and more useful than others.
   In organising we suggest that:

1 — agreeing or setting objectives
4 — defining the subject topic area (with the student?)
5 — structuring the work by suggesting a range of resources and actions
7 — setting a time limit

are most appropriate, though how you use them will depend on whether you have selected the area of work or you and the student have agreed it: (in the latter case, certainly you are unlikely to be able to map the whole learning country in advance (2), to establish the student's existing knowledge exactly, though that is desirable, or to be able to do 8 or 9. 6 is clearly inappropriate given the semi-open-ended nature of the work.

In implementing, you can most usefully use

10 — providing different assignments (unlikely to be specific materials) for the individual
14 and 15 — the latter particularly enabling you to give guidance
17 — because it is in the nature of the work.

Since the student has some freedom of action, 12 and 13 are not very appropriate methods of monitoring and 16 is always dependent on how mature the student is.

In evaluating, 21 would be the most appropriate tool. The other two are not really useful in a normal learning situation of this type.

To reiterate: this does not mean you could *not* use other tools of management; if for example you were very familiar with the area of work suggested you would effectively have (2) available, and this would certainly make it easier for you to sort out relevant resources and to develop unexpected lines of learning on the student's part.

Problem 2 – A number of students on a related project
In organising we suggest

2 – mapping the learning country
3 – establishing skills, etc, *if possible*
4 – defining the topic contents
7 – setting a time limit (overall only)
9 – clear knowledge of possible lines of discovery.

All are essential in planning the project since you are dealing with a group of people each exploring an undetermined part of a large area. It is therefore difficult to agree minimum goals for each one (1), or to predetermine where they go (5, 6, 8). You can only give yourself information in advance which will enable *you* to respond when monitoring their actual work. You might be able to use 5 if you wish to *limit* the area of work.

In implementing:

11 – would be nice but is only possible on a restricted project or if you are producing outline assignments.
14, 16 and possibly 17 are the most likely forms of monitoring, so long as you do not rely on 16 alone; the use of 14 (spot checks) will depend on how thoroughly you have organised to start with.

In evaluating, 21 is really the only possibility, don't you agree? The basic problem is that unless you want to *dictate* what goes on, you can only brief yourself, plan the overall area of work and thence be in a position to respond to and guide the students' work.

Problem 3 — Student choice of work, possibly within an overall range of possibilities
In organising the most useful tools are likely to be

5 — structuring the environment, which may to some extent control range of choices
7 — setting a time limit which, if the student is competent to organise this work, may determine the scope of what he tries to do.

Since he has the choice, 1—4 are not possible; 6, 8 and 9 are inappropriate.

In implementing, the most useful tools may be

14 — because you need to find out what he is doing to influence it
17, 18 — because this is the description of (as opposed to a pre-prescription for) what the student is learning.

You cannot build in feedback in advance since you do not know what is being done nor can you guarantee to provide appropriate materials. You may be able to use tutorials as diagnostic instruments (15).

In evaluating: 21 may once more be the major possible tool (but what criteria will you use to judge?) although if you can establish what the student feels his goals are, by monitoring his work, you may be able to test their achievement (20).

The problem with 'student choice' is that you can rarely manage it in advance, except through structuring the environment in which he chooses; you have to use monitoring to discover what he is doing and then work out how to assess and evaluate it.

Problem 4: An agreed contract
In organising we suggest that

1 — is essential as the basis of the contract
2 — needs to have been done before you even start
3 — as always, is desirable but not always attainable
7 — is useful as a tool for guidance — how long may the student expect to be able to take, both as a whole and on individual parts of the work?
8 — you may find useful, if you have done 2 properly
9 — you need.

You may feel that 4 is desirable but it may also be too restrictive and needs to be considered carefully before you use it, as does 5. After all the essence of a contract is to put some responsibility on the student for organising his own learning within a generally agreed framework.

In implementing
10 — may be useful advance provision since the success of contract work often depends on the students having supportive assignments at crucial points
11 — *might* be useful if you can do it, as might 15
13 or 16 — (depending on your judgement of the student) are essential since you must have regular feedback as to how the student is getting on. 17 and/or 18 are also essential given the limited freedom of choice the student has.

In evaluating

20 — should be practicable
21 — may or may not be practicable depending on the nature of the work
19 — is unlikely to be a good tool since a contract implies that it must be completed to be properly judged.

Problem 5 — using a structured work scheme
In organising

1 – 6 – are *all* essential prerequisites for the design and use
of a structured scheme — by its nature it has been
organised in advance
7   – is optional
8 and 9 – by their nature are inappropriate tools.

In implementing

11 – is very desirable (different levels of material)
12 and 13 – are essential for it to work, and are the main
monitoring tools
17 and 18 – (the latter is essential) are useful
14, 15 and 16 – are less appropriate though they do have
some uses.

In evaluating 19 and 20 are the major methods.

By its nature a structured scheme is a very closely managed
pattern of work and much of that work needs to be done
before it is ever used.

Appendix 1. Information index

This is intended at one time to undertake the function of a working bibliography and to provide an example of the descriptive/topic index described in Chapter 7. Please note that because of its special function it has slight modifications.

1. Only the elements of the books described that are relevant to this book's subject are indexed.
2. The 'level of difficulty' has been reduced to a simple code:
   A = books useful for all teachers interested in the subject
   S = books useful mainly for those who wish to acquire more specialised and deeper knowledge of that aspect.
3. Since there is no 'collection' to refer to, the 'location reference' column has been used to show the location, within the book concerned, of the information relevant to that particular topic.
4. Since the index also functions as an internal index to this book there is an overall index sheet indicating the pages on which that topic is discussed.

Otherwise the index is typical and is in three sections.
   (i) a topic list which can form the basis of a bigger index on resource-oriented work if you wish to build it up. The topics included as 'cards' in this book are in italic.
   (ii) a topic index in alphabetical order designed so that it can be copied or cut out.
   (iii) a descriptive index of all information items referred to in the topic index, in alphabetical order of titles.

Topic list
Overleaf a list of topics is given, together with appropriate references in this book.

Aims
Analysis
Assessment procedures
Classroom management
Control of learning
Definition of resources
Display
Evaluation of activities
Goals
Independent learning
Indexing
Individualised learning
Innovation
Learner analysis
Learning situation analysis
Management of learning
Management of resources
Material formats
Media characteristics
Monitoring
Objectives
Pacing
Patterns of work
Presentation
Problems of assessment
Projects
Questioning
Resource-based work
Retrieval
Selection of media
Sequencing instruction
Storage of resources
Structuring of materials
Systematic approaches
Task analysis
Teacher as manager
Teaching aids
Teaching/learning strategies
Testing

Topic index

AIMS	Int	Ref
Implementing individualised learning	A	Ch 2
Educational technology in		
curriculum development	A	pp 19–28
Coal analysis	A	All

ANALYSIS	Int	Ref
Implementing individualised learning	A	All
Management of learning	A	Sect 1
Algorithm writer's guide	S	Ch 1

ASSESSMENT PROCEDURES	Int	Ref
Techniques and problems of assessment	S	Chs 1–8
Record keeping in the progressive		
primary school	A	Pts 1, 2
Teaching mixed ability classes	A	Ch 8

DEFINITION OF RESOURCES	Int	Ref
Implementing individualised learning	A	pp 102-103
Learning resources – an argument		
for schools	A	Sect 1

DISPLAY	Int	Ref
Implementing individualised learning	A	pp 120-122
Designing for visual aids	A	Pts 2, 3

EVALUATION OF ACTIVITIES	Int	Ref
Implementing individualised learning	A	Ch 9
Constructing achievement tests	S	Ch 6, 7
Management of learning	A	Chs 14–16
Educational technology in curriculum development	A	pp 130–156
Techniques and problems of assessment	S	Ch 15
Record keeping in the progressive primary school	A	Pts 1, 2

GOALS	Int	Ref
Implementing individualised learning		Ch 2
Goal analysis	A	All
Management of learning	A	Chs 3–5
Educational technology in curriculum development	A	pp 34–41
Objectives in curriculum design	S	All
Stating behavioural objectives for classroom use	A	All

INDEXING	Int	Ref
Implementing individualised learning	A	pp 107-110
School library resource centre	A	Ch 9
Learning resources? – an argument for schools	A	Sect 4.1

INDIVIDUALISED LEARNING	Int	Ref
Implementing individualised learning	A	All
Resources for learning	A	All
Management of learning	A	Ch 8
Teaching mixed ability classes	A	Ch 2

INNOVATION	Int	Ref
Implementing individualised learning	A	All
Resources for learning	A	All
Management of learning	A	Chs 1—2
Objectives in curriculum design	S	All

LEARNER ANALYSIS	Int	Ref
Implementing individualised learning	A	pp 65-66
Teaching mixed ability classes	A	Chs 4, 6, 7

LEARNING SITUATION ANALYSIS	Int	Ref
Implementing individualised learning	A	Chs 1-5
Management of learning	A	Chs 6—9

MANAGEMENT OF LEARNING	Int	Ref
Implementing individualised learning	A	All
Management of learning	A	All
Teaching mixed ability classes	A	Chs 1—9

MATERIAL FORMATS	Int	Ref
Implementing individualised learning	A	pp 143-146
Algorithm writer's guide	S	All

MEDIA CHARACTERISTICS	Int	Ref
Implementing individualised learning	A	pp 146-152
Designing for visual aids	A	Pt 2
Educational technology in curriculum development	A	pp 103—30
Selection and use of instructional media	S	Chs 2—10

MONITORING	Int	Ref
Implementing individualised learning	A	pp 91-99
Techniques and problems of		
assessment	S	Ch 9
Record keeping in the progressive		
primary school	S	Pt 2, 3

OBJECTIVES	Int	Ref
Implementing individualised learning	A	Ch 2
Educational technology in		
curriculum development	A	pp 19–70
Goal analysis	A	All
Management of learning	A	Ch 5
Objectives in curriculum design	S	All
Stating behavioural objectives for		
classroom use	A	All

PATTERNS OF WORK	Int	Ref
Implementing individualised learning	A	Ch 6
Educational technology in		
curriculum development	A	pp 71–102
Resources in schools	A	Ch 4

PROBLEMS OF ASSESSMENT	Int	Ref
Implementing individualised learning	A	Chs 6, 9
Techniques and problems of		
assessment	S	Chs 9–16

PROJECTS	Int	Ref
Implementing individualised learning	A	pp 87-90; App 3
Techniques and problems of assessment	S	Ch 7

QUESTIONING	Int	Ref
Implementing individualised learning	A	pp 160-162
Techniques and problems of assessment	S	Chs 1−3

RESOURCE BASED WORK	Int	Ref
Implementing individualised learning	A	All
Resources for learning	A	All
Learning resources? − an argument for schools	A	Sect 4.4

RETRIEVAL	Int	Ref
Implementing individualised learning	A	pp 113-120
Resources in schools	A	Ch 5

SEQUENCING OF INSTRUCTION	Int	Ref
Implementing individualised learning	A	Ch 8
Educational technology in curriculum development	A	pp 71−102
Good frames and bad	S	Ch 3
Algorithm writer's guide	S	All

STORAGE OF RESOURCES	Int	Ref
Implementing individualised learning	A	pp 110-113
School library resource centre	A	Ch 10

STRUCTURING OF MATERIALS	Int	Ref
Implementing individualised learning	A	Ch 8
Good frames and bad	S	Chs 2, 5
Algorithm writer's guide	S	All
Objectives in curriculum design	S	Ch 10

SYSTEMATIC APPROACHES	Int	Ref
Implementing individualised learning	A	All
Selection and use of instructional media	S	Ch 1
Management of learning	A	All
Objectives in curriculum design	S	Ch 10

TASK ANALYSIS	Int	Ref
Implementing individualised learning	A	Ch 3
Educational technology in curriculum development	A	pp 79–93
Management of learning	A	Ch 3

TEACHER AS MANAGER	Int	Ref
Implementing individualised learning	A	Chs 4, 9
Management of learning	A	Chs 2, 16

TEACHING/LEARNING STRATEGIES	Int	Ref
Implementing individualised learning	A	Chs 1-4, 9
Educational technology in curriculum development	A	pp 93–102

TEACHING AIDS	Int	Ref
Management of learning	A	Ch 7
Selection and use of instructional media	S	Chs 2–10
Designing for visual aids	A	All

TESTING	Int	Ref
Implementing individualised learning	A	Ch 9
Constructing achievement tests	S	All
Educational technology in curriculum development	A	pp 60–70
Management of learning	A	Chs 14–16

Descriptive index
The following index represents card entries which may be copied if desired.

(THE) ALGORITHM WRITER'S GUIDE

D M Wheatley & D W Unwin   Longman   1972

Contents — A practical guide to the writing of algorithmic procedures as a means of enabling people to solve problems. Most of the illustrations are from industrial or domestic situations but the principles apply to educational ones also. Algorithms are decision-making procedures (of which an example may be found on pp166-175 in the book you are reading). The guide discusses what an algorithm consists of, how to produce one and what the problems of use are. It gives some guidance on the layout and visual design.

Suitable for — Teachers particularly interested in problem-solving procedures.

Index under — Analysis; Material formats; Sequencing instruction; Structuring materials.

CONSTRUCTING ACHIEVEMENT TESTS

N E Gronlund   Prentice-Hall   1968

Contents – Intended as a practical guide to constructing tests of achievement for students, this was written for the American market but is useful in British conditions. Its advice is strongly linked to the formation of measurable learning goals and it covers in detail the general planning of tests, the construction of multiple-choice questions, and essay tests, the problems of administering and evaluating such tests. It gives some guidance on ways of determining test validity and reliability.

Suitable for – Teachers with special interest in, and some experience of, formal achievement testing.

Index under – Evaluation of activities; Testing.

DESIGNING FOR VISUAL AIDS

A Wright   Studio Vista   1970

Contents – Illustrated discussion of how to design the visual elements in information and learning materials. Fairly superficial but provides useful advice on visual design in various media, which can be used by the teacher.

Pt 1: is general reading on 'learning and teaching'. It is worth reading as background.

Pt 2: deals very briefly with visuals in various media.

Pt 3: is concerned with the design of educational visual materials and will be found valuable by most teachers needing to produce student material. It takes into account appropriateness of the visual design to content and the learner's problems of interpreting and responding to what he sees.

Index under – Displays; Media characteristics; Teaching aids.

EDUCATIONAL TECHNOLOGY IN CURRICULUM DEVELOPMENT

D Rowntree   Harper & Row   1974

Contents — As may be guessed from the title this is a wide ranging but general book. It deals with systematic processes in educational development, in particular aims and objectives of various kinds; the evaluation of objectives and their achievement; problems of designing learning to suit different situations; the functions of various media in facilitating learning and the problems of selecting appropriate media; problems of evaluation. Teachers unfamiliar with the term 'educational technology' need not be frightened off since its nature is briefly discussed as are the problems of innovation generally. Specific sections and sub-sections may be found of practical help, and the book has therefore been widely topic-indexed.

Suitable for — All teachers interested in innovation.

Index under — Aims; Evaluation of activities; Goals; Media characteristics; Objectives; Patterns of work; Selection of media; Sequencing instructions; Task analysis; Teaching strategies.

GOAL ANALYSIS

R F Mager   (in UK) Pitman   1972

Contents – A chatty but very useful approach to the problems of analysing and constructing general learning goals. It discusses in detail reasons for setting goals, the problems of identifying and avoiding fuzzy goal statements, provides a practical guide on how to write goals and what pitfalls the goal-writer may encounter. Useful but needs to be read right through.

Suitable for – Any teacher seriously involved in individualising learning.

Index under – Aims; Goals. Objectives.

GOOD FRAMES AND BAD

S Meyer Markle   Wiley   2nd ed 1969

Contents – This is basically a specialist instruction book for people concerned with writing learning programmes but it also has sections that are useful to the teacher-writer of material. It covers problems of presenting various types of information (irrespective of medium) and of eliciting valid responses.
The most useful sections are:
Chapter 2 – basic elements, defines ways of eliciting responses from a user of material, in particular discussing the methods and problems of prompting (ie, helping the user to learn).
Chapter 3 – 'Systematic approaches to design' discusses possible ways of ordering material information to facilitate learning.
Chapter 5 – 'Editing' contains a useful section on establishing that responses are relevant to the learning and on the avoidance of responses that may be relevant but do not advance learning.

Index under – Sequencing of instruction; Structuring of materials.

LEARNING RESOURCES? – AN ARGUMENT FOR SCHOOLS

W J K Davies   Council for Educational Technology   1975

Contents – This is one of the CET Guidelines series and is intended for schools and colleges considering the organisation of their resources at institution level. It consists of four sections; a definition of resources; a discussion on why a school may want to organise its resources; a discussion on how to implement its wishes; a series of information summaries. For individual teachers Section 1 and information summaries 4.1 and 4.4. (Indexing; Implications for individualised work) may prove useful. Section 1 in particular explores resource definition in some depth.

Index under – Definition of resources; Indexing; Resource-based work.

° (THE) MANAGEMENT OF LEARNING

I K Davies   McGraw Hill   1971

Contents – The book sets out not to teach teachers how to teach, but to give them specific tools they can use to make their own decisions. After a general introduction it provides sections on planning objectives and analysis; organising methods; selecting appropriate tactics, groupings and aids; problems of leading students rather than directing them; and of managing and evaluating the learning process.

Suitable for – All teachers interested in individualising learning.

Index under – Evaluation of activities; Individualised learning; Innovation; Learning situation analysis; Management of learning; Objectives; Systematic approaches; Task analysis; Testing.

OBJECTIVES IN CURRICULUM DESIGN

I K Davies   McGraw Hill   1976

Contents – A very detailed discussion of the place and limitations of goals and objectives in curriculum planning. It covers their history, the problems and advantages of objectives; the characteristics of various specific types of objectives. It then discusses the alternatives to objectives, considering both 'open' and 'closed' approaches to the curriculum. This is not a primer on writing objectives but a very thorough and perceptive study.

Suitable for – Teachers wishing to think deeply about problems of objectives at school and class level.

Index under – Goals; Innovation; Objectives; Structuring of materials; Systematic approaches.

PREPARING INSTRUCTIONAL OBJECTIVES

R F Mager   (in UK) Pitman   2nd ed 1975

Contents — This book is a piece of self-instructional learning material which teaches the reader to examine and apply the author's methods of producing precise, measurable objectives. It was written for both teachers and instructors so that some of the examples may appear irrelevant to the school situation and it was also written for the American market so that some idioms may be unfamiliar to British readers. It includes self-checking tests at the end.

Suitable for — All teachers wishing to define specific objectives.

Index under — Objectives; Testing.

RECORD KEEPING IN THE PROGRESSIVE
PRIMARY SCHOOL

P Rance   Ward Lock Educational   1975

Contents – Although written for primary schools many of the ideas and ways of recording progress are applicable to individualised work at secondary level. The book has 3 parts.
1. Background information: why keep records; the problems of record keeping in various teaching and learning situations.
2. Types of records: descriptions of various methods of record keeping, with notes on their characteristics.
3. Illustrated examples of various recording procedures: a useful section, though some of the examples shown are applicable only to primary schools.

Suitable for – All teachers interested in individualised and resource-oriented work.

Index under – Assessment procedures; Evaluating of activities; Monitoring.

RESOURCES FOR LEARNING

L C Taylor   Penguin   2nd ed 1972

Contents — A thoughtful study of methods of work, mainly in secondary schools, arising out of the author's work with the Nuffield Foundation. It considers various teaching methods, describes work going on in America, Russia and Sweden in connection with innovation in teaching and surveys some past attempts to innovate. It then discusses ways of trying to improve learning within the constraints of the school system and advocates the production and use of learning packages of various types. It is useful as general back-ground stimulus reading and does not set out to be a practical guide.

Suitable for — All teachers.

Index under — Individualised learning; Innovation; Resource-based work.

RESOURCES IN SCHOOLS

R P A Edwards   Evans   1973

Contents – This book discusses the reasons for and problems of establishing resource centres in schools. It is written from the librarian/provision of hardware and software viewpoint and contains –

(i) general and rapidly dating information on types of apparatus, both reprographic and audio-visual presentation devices

(ii) the physical planning of centralised resource areas, based mainly on experiments in various Leicestershire schools

(iii) 'Using the Resource Centre' (Ch 4). This is a general consideration of ways in which a central resource area might be used as an integral part of an individualised learning situation and contains a number of useful suggestions and ideas – though they are written from the point of view of a resource organiser rather than a teacher

(iv) retrieval systems (Ch 5) provides descriptions of various 'systems', in particular the conventional Dewey based one, OCCI, and punched card systems

(v) short comments on staffing, outside links and finance which are likely to be of interest only to resource organisers.

The book is not generally of much use to the classroom teacher but Chapters 4 and 5 can provide food for thought.

Suitable for – All interested teachers.

Index under – Patterns of work; Retrieval.

SCHOOL LIBRARY RESOURCE CENTRE

M Allan   Crosby Lockwood Staples   1974

Contents — Written from a librarian's point of view and studying the problems of setting up a library-based resource centre at school level; applicable mainly to secondary schools and also to colleges of further education. The book assumes that a library is the natural focus for resource organisation and covers in detail ways of classifying, subject indexing, storing and preparing materials for retrieval. The classroom teacher may find Chapter 2 interesting and Chapters 9 and 10 helpful in his own work.

Suitable for — Professional school librarians; teacher librarians; ancillary assistants.

Index under — Indexing; Storage.

SELECTION AND USE OF INSTRUCTIONAL MEDIA

A J Romisowski   Kogan Page   1974

Contents — The book starts with an introduction to systematic approaches to learning design written in a fairly technical manner and so mainly useful for those already familiar with the language — which also applies to the following section of factors and characteristics affecting choice of media. There follow eight useful sections on specific visual, audio and audio-visual media, discussing each in turn and providing guidance on when they may be useful. The approach is biased toward instruction rather than student-oriented learning.

Suitable for — Teachers wishing to use varied media and prepared to study the problems in depth.

Index under — Media; Systematic approaches; Teaching aids.

STATING BEHAVIOURAL OBJECTIVES FOR CLASSROOM INSTRUCTION

N E Gronlund   Collier-Macmillan   1970

Contents – This small book is intended as a practical primer for teachers wanting to write objectives for use in teaching and testing. It discusses the use of goals and objectives in defining outcomes; gives guidance in how to produce objectives, at various levels, which will be measurable; and explains how to use objectives both in planning and testing. It includes a number of useful tables.

Suitable for – All teachers interested in goal-oriented work.

Index under – Goals; Objectives; Testing (Ch 7).

TEACHING MIXED ABILITY CLASSES

A V Kelly   Harper & Row   1974

Contents – A general discussion, from the viewpoint of a teacher-trainer, of problems involved in mixed-ability work. It is written at a theoretical rather than a practical guide level but provides useful background reading on:
(i) the problems of various teaching strategies (individual and group assignments; team teaching; groupings)
(ii) teacher-pupil relationships especially where slow learners are concerned
(iii) assessment at the top end of the secondary school.
It should be emphasised that the discussion is general rather than specific.

Suitable for – All teachers wanting background reading.

Index under – Assessment; Individualised learning; Learner analysis; Management of learning.

TECHNIQUES AND PROBLEMS OF ASSESSMENT

H G MacIntosh   Edward Arnold   1974

Contents – The book is a symposium of contributions by a number of writers and its standard is not always constant. It is however, intended as a practical guide to assessment in educational situations and is divided into two sections.
(i) Techniques: covers in some detail the problems of test questioning of various kinds and also examines the problems of assessing practical project work.
(ii) Problems: this discusses in detail problems of all main types of classroom assessment. As a general primer this book would be useful to all classroom teachers seriously involved in individualised or resource oriented work.

Suitable for – Teachers wishing to study assessment seriously.

Index under – Assessment procedures; Assessment problems; Evaluation of activities: Monitoring; Projects; Questioning.

Appendix 2. Structured teaching material examples

These samples are intended for two purposes: to show *some* possible ways of structuring *teaching* materials for active learning, and to act as practice exercises for those wishing to identify features and problems discussed in Chapter 8.

There are six samples. For each one you are invited to identify:

(1) What is the student expected to do?
(2) What response is he required to make?
(3) How is that response elicited?
(4) If any clues or prompts are given and, if so, what?
(5) If any directions are given and, if so, what part they play?
(6) How is feedback provided to student and/or teacher?
(7) What controls can you identify that would make the learning effective or ineffective?

Suggested answers will be found on the pages immediately following the originals. It should be noted that because of the limitations of this format all are in 'paper' form but this does not imply that you can structure only 'paper-based' material.

Example 1: A small learning step involving teacher monitoring.

Read these words.

......first

.....bird

girl......

...skirt

shirt...

What sound does this word family make? Tell your teacher.

Note: The page shown is part of a structured booklet using various existing skills to learn new material. In the original, the letters 'ir' are printed in a second colour·

Source: Signpost Word Families, copyright A Westrope and H Tross.

Example 2. Material to consolidate and develop a previous piece of learning

Source IRMA © St Albans PLC

Reading Sheet I   Sound a

I.   Make sure you can read all these words. Draw
      pictures of 5 of them:

at	Sam	sat	ham	bag
can	fat	man	lap	pan
jam	wag	an	rat	gag
tap	bad	mad	fan	sad
had	gap	jazz	sat	map

2.   Add one letter to make each word :

-at	-ag	ta-	ha-	va-
pa-	-ad	-ap	ca-	ja-

3.   Put the right label by each picture :

      fat   can   fan   pan   sad   cat

4.   Use 5 of these words in sentences of your own.

Example 3: Response structured teaching material with
immediate feedback for student

4. You might have some of these answers:
  (i) Fix a direction by the position of the sun, moon or stars.
 	
  (ii) Use a compass — where is north?
 	
  (iii) Use a distant landmark.
	Well, did you have conclusions like that?
	  (i) The sun moves, so does the moon and most of the stars. (One star does not seem to — the Pole star.) So it depends on the time of day as to which direction you face to see the sun or moon or particular stars — which is not very useful for *fixing* a direction unless you know the exact time.
	
	  (ii) If you have a compass, this is the best method, it *fixes an initial direction.* What is the initial direction? In what direction does the compass needle point.

5. North. The magnetic north, but this is very close to the North Pole.	We usually take the northerly direction as our I . . . . . L direction. (Fill in the missing word).
6. INITIAL	(iii) Which way do we turn, to the right or left? Well we can say face north, turn 30° to the right. But it would be easier if we all agreed to turn the same way, clockwise or anti-clockwise, left or right. If I turn clock-wise, am I turning right or left?

7. Right.	Navigators have agreed to turn and measure their directions in a clockwise sense from north. To face in a direction of 123° then, means: (i) face north (ii) turn through 123° in a clockwise sense. 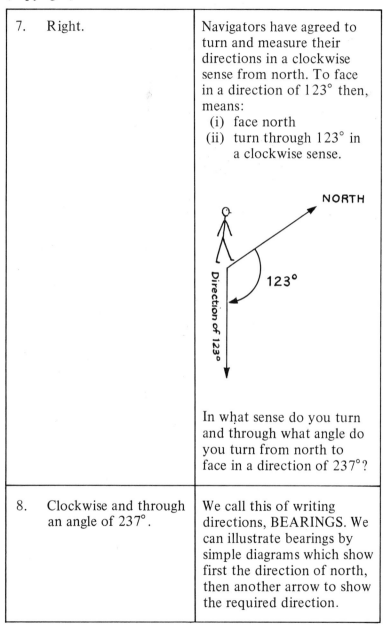 In what sense do you turn and through what angle do you turn from north to face in a direction of 237°?
8. Clockwise and through an angle of 237°.	We call this of writing directions, BEARINGS. We can illustrate bearings by simple diagrams which show first the direction of north, then another arrow to show the required direction.

Example 4: Response structured practice material with immediate feedback for students

15. 057°
     (How close were you?
     An answer between
     056° and 058° can
     be correct.)
	What bearing does this show?
	
	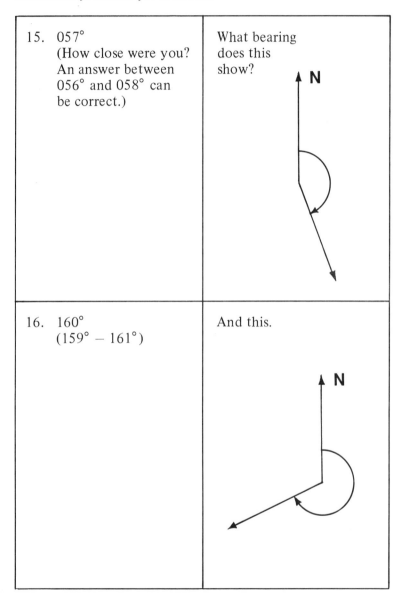

16. 160° (159° − 161°)	And this.

Source: City of Birmingham Structured Mathematics
       Scheme (copyright)

17. 245°
     (244° − 246°)
     (Were you accurate ?)
	And this.
	
	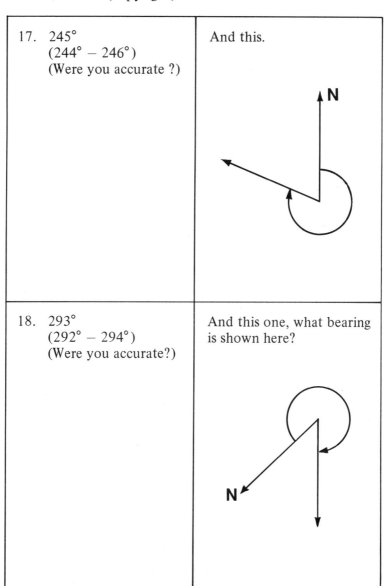

18. 293°
     (292° − 294°)
     (Were you accurate?)
	And this one, what bearing
	is shown here?

Example 5

To test for protein by using Millon's reagent
(1) *Answer sheet*
Remove this Answer sheet and fill it in as you work through
the program.

Name . . . .

1.   . . . . is the chemical which is used to test
      for protein.
2.   Before a change can be seen in the protein powder, the
      test tube containing the protein powder and the
      Millon's reagent needs to be . . . . . .
3.   After this the protein powder changes to a . . . .
      colour.
4.   . . . . is then heated with crushed peas.
5.   This is to find if the crushed peas contain . . . .
6.   THERE IS/THERE IS NOT a similar colour change in
      both the protein powder and the crushed peas when
      they are heated with Millon's reagent. (Cross out
      the wrong answer).
7.   This shows that peas are a food which DO CONTAIN/
      DO NOT CONTAIN the foodstuff protein. (Cross out
      the wrong answer).

(2) *Test for protein*

Check you have the apparatus as shown in the diagram.

Source: Simple Food Test, J Goodfellow. © St. Albans PLC

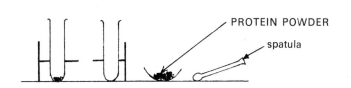

Use the spatula to put enough protein powder in one of the test tubes to cover the bottom of the test tube.

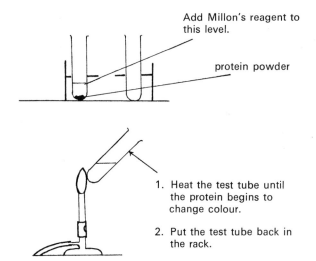

Answer the questions by completing the first sentence on the answer sheet.

Questions:

(a)   Which chemical have you used to test for protein?
(b)   Before you can see a change in the protein powder, what must you do after adding the chemical?
(c)   What colour do you then see in the protein powder?

Example 6: Response structured material using visual discrimination as main stimulus
This comprises three pages from a booklet on identifying various features on churches.

Cruciform   15

Houses and churches have walls and roofs, windows and doors. But what does a church have, usually at one end, that a house does not?

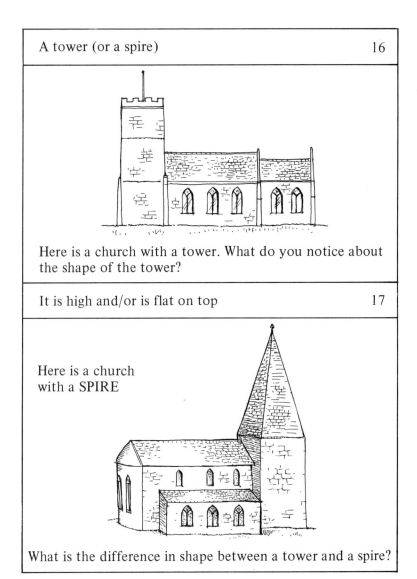

| A tower (or a spire) | 16 |

Here is a church with a tower. What do you notice about the shape of the tower?

| It is high and/or is flat on top | 17 |

Here is a church
with a SPIRE

What is the difference in shape between a tower and a spire?

Answers to Example 1

1. The student is expected to identify the sound made by a particular digraph.

2. He is required to sound the digraph and to let another person hear him.

3. Response is elicited by clueing the stimulus material and by an instruction.

4. Clues are given by colour-coding the digraph.

5. Directions tell the student what to do and ensure monitoring takes place.

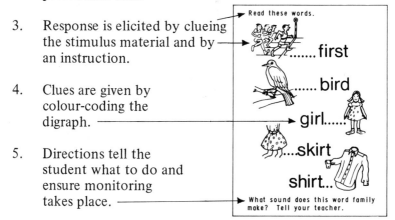

Read these words.

.... first

...... bird

girl.....

....skirt

shirt..

What sound does this word family make? Tell your teacher.

6. Feedback is provided:
    to the *teacher* by hearing the student
    to the *student* by the teacher's comments.

Answers to Example 2

1. The student is expected to do a series of tasks to consolidate his understanding of and ability to apply a single vowel sound.

2. Varied: he completes words; identifies words; uses words; to show he knows their meaning.

3. By instructions.

4. Clues are given by substituting dashes in Q.2 in the appropriate places.

5. Directions tell the student what to do.

6. Feedback has to be provided by the teacher checking on what is going on.

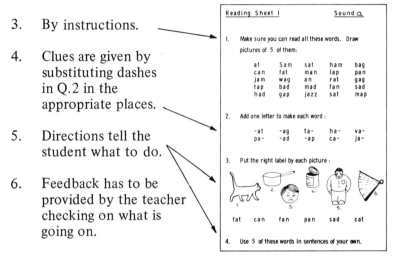

7. There are no controls implicit in the material so, to ensure it is effective the teacher must monitor what the student is doing.

Answers to Example 3

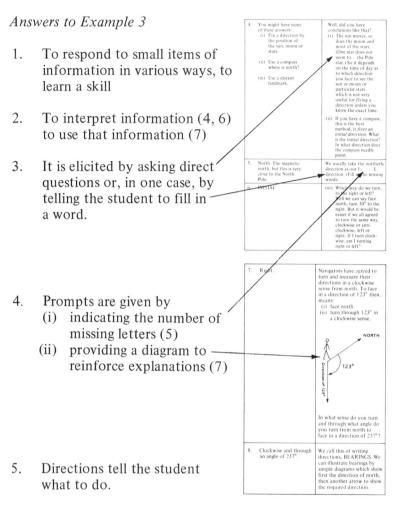

1.   To respond to small items of information in various ways, to learn a skill

2.   To interpret information (4, 6) to use that information (7)

3.   It is elicited by asking direct questions or, in one case, by telling the student to fill in a word.

4.   Prompts are given by
     (i)   indicating the number of missing letters (5)
     (ii) providing a diagram to reinforce explanations (7)

5.   Directions tell the student what to do.

6.   Feedback is provided to the *student* by giving him the answers to the questions asked.

7.   The structure of the material controls the learning; you could suggest the student uses a sheet of paper to cover parts of the material to avoid him inadvertently seeing answers in advance but this is not important.

Answers to Example 4

1. The student is expected to practise
    working out bearings.

2. He works out the bearings from diagrams

3. by instructions.

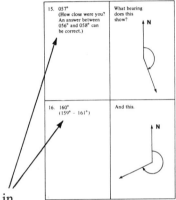

4. No clues or prompts except in
    helping him judge his answer (18).

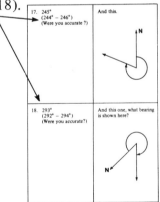

5. Directions are replaced by
    questions.

6. Feedback is provided to the
    student by giving him the
    answers to a question before
    he does the next one.

7. As for 3.

Answers to Example 5

1. Student is expected to carry out an experiment and note the results.

2. He is required to observe and to note his observations.

3. They are elicited by questioning.

4. The diagrams are used as prompts.

5. Directions tell the student what to do and alert him as to what should happen.

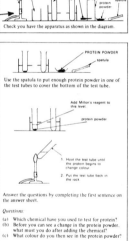

6. Feedback is provided *to the student* by
   (i) giving him diagrammatic checks
   (ii) providing a framework in which his answers must make sense (the answer sheet).

7. Control is a problem. You need to be certain that the student is competent to carry out the sort of task involved and that he can interpret instructions.

Answers to Example 6

1. The student is expected to look at the sketches and use them to answer the questions.

2. He is expected to identify the features known as towers and spires and to distinguish between them.

3. It is elicited by questions related directly to the stimulus information.

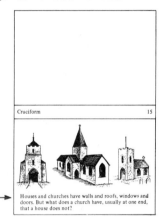

4. Question structure on page 15 is a prompt. ──────────────▶

5. Directions are not used.

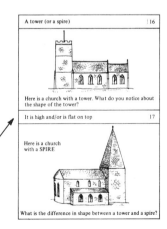

6. Feedback is given to the *student* by providing the answer to each question before he carries on.

7. The internal structure plus trials give control.

Appendix 3. A method of planning individualised work

A method of planning individualised work in general (mapping the learning country): all work involving a series of assignments and/or a spread of subject matter, to be successful, requires similar approaches in that you need:

(1) to determine the overall and detail minimum goals in terms of: reasons for undertaking the work; information content area; identification of any particular content skills (eg, information-handling) that you wish the student to develop

(2) to define the boundaries of the subject matter (knowledge and/or content skills involved) and to sort out the important items within the overall topic

(3) to overcome the organisational problems (1) and (2) imply; viz: —
  — to identify subject matter elements that may lend themselves to development of content or learning skills
  — to assemble/acquire/produce relevant resources and the assignments relating to them
  — to identify areas of difficulty — and equally to find those areas where you will not need to do much to help the students!
  — to identify areas where sequence of work may be important.

And, clearly, you may wish either to do these yourself or to involve your students in working out the project/contract; equally you may want to keep the overall plan to yourself or to have the relevant information (goals, extent of the work, etc) displayed for them to see.

The easiest 'way in' for any information-based work scheme is to start by exploring the subject matter and, by doing so, both define the boundaries of the project and identify various problems: if you complain that this is restricting on the student, we would suggest it is not so — though when you work out what might be involved you may deliberately wish to take only a section of work. On the other hand you can always extend the boundaries and it does enable you to search out the implications of any subject topic and to identify the elements such as: subject matter content; areas of difficulty; areas amenable to the development of content and learning skills.

There are various ways of doing this but one of the more useful would seem to be the 'thinking aloud'-type diagram variously known, from its shape and nature, as a mural topic index, a coral diagram, or a subject tree. The two latter terms describe its nature very well since its creation consists in starting from a central root or nucleus and then drawing related 'branches' or 'growths' each working out one aspect of the topic under consideration. You can thus quite quickly get down all sorts of aspects of the subject and as in using a thesaurus, one 'keyword' or phrase is likely to generate another.

The easiest way of learning to do it is to look at an example — in this case of a broad subject topic, WATER (an old favourite). A first attempt might look like this

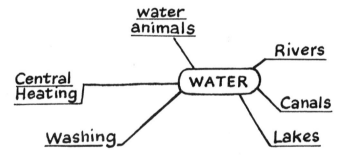

Can you see the problem? — what was it? note down your answer and read on.

If you just scribble down the first words that come, you will soon overcrowd the 'nucleus' and the diagram becomes unmanageable. Suppose you look at the scribble again. You will see the items fall into three groups:

rivers, canals, lakes   — are *places* where water is found
water animals   — are *things living in water*
central heating, washing   — are *uses* of water

If you can identify some major aspects at the start you make the job easier. Look below.

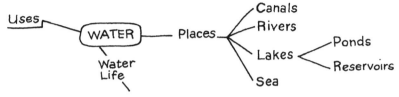

You can see that the idea of 'places' already generates further ideas.

Carry the diagram a little further on the other two aspects and see what you get.

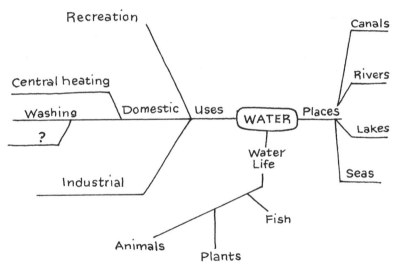

You may well have put a list of *uses* straight on the end of that stem but it is worth noting that, if you get a lot, they may need subdividing themselves as we have done here. Let us think aloud a bit further on part of the 'place' stem: say on canals, rivers and lakes. You can spend a lot of time just pondering but it is probably best to follow the old precept 'don't get it right, get it down' and then to sort it out afterwards. Just think of aspects of each stem under places as listed: canals: rivers: reservoirs.

You may have gone for various aspects . . . for example in rivers you might have any of the following labels or more:

— length, sources, uses, weirs, rapids, waterfalls, bridges
— reservoirs might generate things like uses, dams, pipelines, size, placing
— canals might take in: barges, locks, uses, history, towpaths.

Different people will think of different 'keywords' and these in turn will generate others. In addition you may have just jotted them down as a 'fuzz' of 'twigs' or you may have grouped various aspects together. For example,

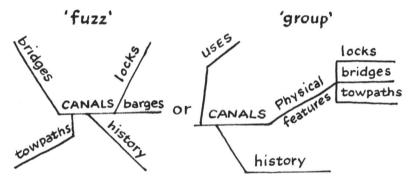

Either is acceptable to start with, but you do need to sort your branches out!

Using 'canals' as an example, work out more detail for *rivers and reservoirs* grouping the labels under various aspects of the place.

Your pattern may look something like this:

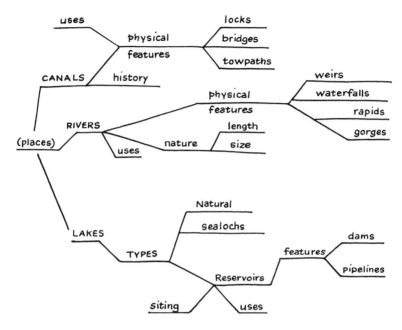

This is only one way of developing: different people will use different 'stems' and so come up with different ideas – but the further you go the more complete your survey of the 'subject matter' country becomes . . . it is just the projection you choose which will determine what the final map looks like! But, however you do it, you are likely to come up with *two* problems. Can you identify them from the diagram above?

However you do it you soon get to a state where:

(a) common elements start appearing on branches.

(b) you start identifying *connections* between different major aspects (eg, recreational and industrial use ◄───► canals as a place).

This is one of the problems of any diagrammatic presentation and only you can decide what you want to do about it.

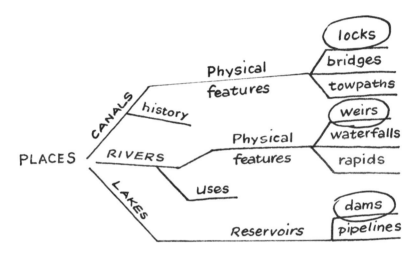

The common elements themselves often give a clue as to what can be done: look at those ringed in the diagram above and say what is common about them?

They all describe some means of controlling the flow of water. Yes? In that case you could extract them and put them all on a new main stem called 'means of controlling flow' or some such . . . just as you could collect 'barges', 'ships', and put them on a stem which you could label 'transport by'. In that case you would get a widespread diagram with a fair number of main branches but one in which you always need to make into connections to obtain a topic area.

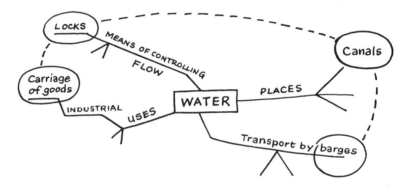

Alternatively you can retain the common items and in some way note the links (we underlined some for instance). What effect would this have?

It would make it easier for you or a student to get the whole picture of any one aspect of the subject matter but would mean a lot of near-duplication of the diagram. So you have eventually to decide whether to retain the duplication which gives you 'instant detail' of one aspect as shown below:

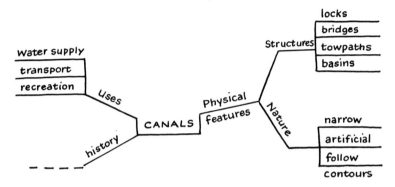

Alternatively you can break the diagram down, which gives you the general picture better but is more difficult in viewing detail. Both methods have their uses: can you identify the major uses for —

(a)   retaining duplication (if need be, in a modified form?)
(b)   reorganising the diagram

Retaining (and expanding) duplication

It is particularly useful if you are wanting to take a comparatively narrow aspect of a general subject topic and study it (or prepare assignments on it) in detail. Quite soon you get to a level where you can isolate out possible areas for assignments and consider their part in the work.

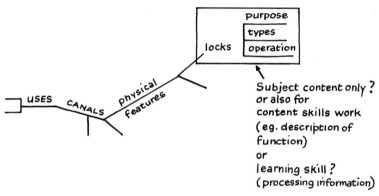

It also gives you a better chance of defining the boundaries of the work — and the extent which you have got by now shows the problem of doing this until you know what is involved. A broad topic like 'water' can only be studied at a general level by students unless you either take a great deal of time or groups study different aspects, so are you going to include everything or just selected aspects? History, uses, features, etc, of canals or just their main characteristics and uses in relation to other forms of waterways? What sort(s) of assignments do you want on this aspect of the subject? Can your students find out how a lock works — in which case you could use that as an assignment to develop skills — or do you have to explain it (demonstrate? teach?). What resources do you have to hand — a canal? a film? photographs? models? Whatever they are you should be able to identify fairly precisely what you are likely to want.

It is particularly useful for students who can then see the immediate ramifications of any particular aspect in which they are interested and a map of this kind can well be used for wall displays, the generation of general descriptions of assignments, etc.

It may, however, be irritating rather than useful if *you* want to sort out the main links between aspects of a subject so that you can decide *how* to approach it. In that case it may be better to reorganise the diagram.

Reorganisation of the original 'thinking aloud' diagram to group common elements is useful mainly for *you* to determine all the main aspects of a general topic area. The diagram below shows the start of a typical 'map'.

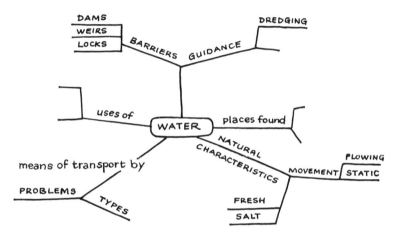

It is more difficult to do since it involves functional classifications and, again, different people may come up with different groupings. But it doesn't matter very much. Why not, do you think?

The exact result doesn't matter so much because much of the value of any 'thinking aloud' exercise lies in the very fact of having thought and then jotted down one's thoughts so that they are not lost. Both forms of 'coral diagrams' are useful as ways of noting and displaying one's ideas in that:

(a) you can organise them as you want
(b) you have a chance to develop aspects you might otherwise have forgotten.

But they are only a way of searching out the content. If we are talking about mapping the learning country, what we have been doing so far is conducting a rough survey and ordering our notes! This may be all you need to do, or you may want to see more clearly just what the implications are for organisation of the work.

If you want to explore this line further, please read on.

You would like to make use of the information provided, to make one or more 'informative maps of the learning country' you are going to explore with your students, or are going to ask them to explore on their own. But what kind of map?

(1) You may just want to provide more organised information about the content — to produce a sort of basic sketch rather than a true map. Turn to page 252.

(2) You may want to provide an indication of where particular learning explorations may take the student — a route map of the country so to speak. And as part of this you want to use it to identify areas of difficulty which the student may encounter. Turn to page 254.

(3) You may want to use it as a tool for checking that items have not been left out of a particular line of enquiry (a detailed guide to ensure that some particular 'piece' of learning country has been fully explored). Turn to page 258.

(1) *Using the basic diagram to provide organised information about work content*

This is probably the simplest, assuming that you know what the students are to do.

1. Select from the diagram the area(s) you want to study.

2. Find out (hopefully from your index and experience) what resource materials you have that are relevant, and at the right level of difficulty.

3. On the *'map'*, in the appropriate place, note useful information (ie, the library reference numbers for useful things stored there: location references for items in your own collection; notes on environmental sources). This can of course be either for your own information, in your project/contract design notes or it can be for students.

4. Display it as part of the content 'map' on a classroom wall for example (libraries sometimes do this) — and, if you want, get your students to build it up.

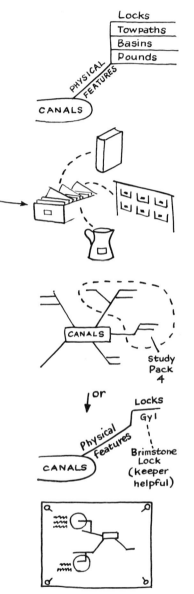

5. Use the information to help design *appropriate* assignments (in the sense you know the content information will be there) NB: but watch for safety factors, etc.

look for "CANALS & THEIR HISTORY" in the index.
In chapter 3.. it says
~~~~ ~~~ ~~~
What do you ...?

or

Go to Brimstone lock and watch a boat locking through.
What sequence of events....

(2) *Making a route map*

There may be occasions in which you want to guide the student over a particular learning route or routes — or indeed may yourself want to establish any essential connections between various pieces of learning so as to see if one task depends on the successful completion of any other. Learning involving content skills, such as mathematics, or learning skills, such as ability to summarise information, is an area where this technique may be useful.

The technicalities are simple in that if you can break down the learning content (in terms of information or skill) into smallish areas, you need only to arrange them so that they follow on one from another. Indeed if you have a 'coral' diagram well worked out, you can partly flow-diagram it simply by 'opening out' the main stems and tracing their branches out in linear fashion. And you can do it vertically or horizontally so long as you remember that if *flows*, so you need to show connections by means, for example, of arrowed lines.

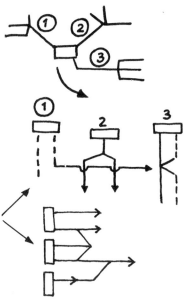

But then the technicalities of driving a car are simple too . . . it is the practicalities that matter and they come from practice and experience. In other words you are the only person who can turn the idea into something useful for you; it is your subject knowledge and experience which enable you to see that a student cannot do Y before he has done X and V, whereas Z depends on neither of them; so then you can say:

The advantages are that you can more easily locate points of possible difficulty, for example where a number of routes come together or where future progress depends on mastering something particular, but like any other skill it needs practice to make a useful tool. You might like, before we go on, to look at a few examples.

On p 67 you will find a simple flow diagram built up to show development of an idea and two different ways of achieving the same end.

On p 187 and p 257 are two others:

(1)   a section of a content skills chart, showing how it can indicate connections
(2)   an outline flow chart of the tasks needed to organise a project.

So a 'map' of this kind is only really helpful if you can define your goals and the content involved in reaching them. If you are happy to do that, please go on.

If you can do that, then the following conventions may prove useful to you for putting your ideas on paper.

Prerequisite
(1) You need to have identified at least most of the subject areas you want to cover before you start — whether you do it by thinking aloud, by borrowing or some other method.

(2) Put each area or skill down on a scrap of paper or card (so you can move them around).

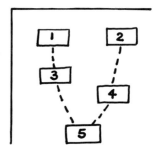

(3) Sort the cards into the order(s) you think they should be in and lay them out on a large sheet of paper. For each area or skill task use the following questions to establish connections.

(a) Does the 'area' or 'task' imply that a student has to be able to do something else first (as a prerequisite)?
(b) Are any areas (or routes, as they emerge)
    — separate from each other
    — coming to junctions?

NB as with thinking-aloud diagrams of any sort, you may well find additional skills, etc, being identified — so put them in; you may also find your original 'plan' is not working out so that you need to modify the diagram — but that is why you used cards.

(4) Convert your 'cards' into a single diagram. Common conventions are:

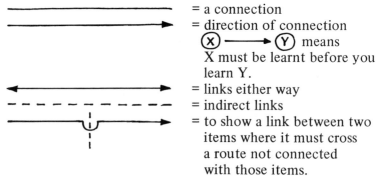

(5) Examine points where a number of lines converge, or where a task has to be mastered.

(a) to see if there is special difficulty
(b) to consider what if anything needs to be done to help students.

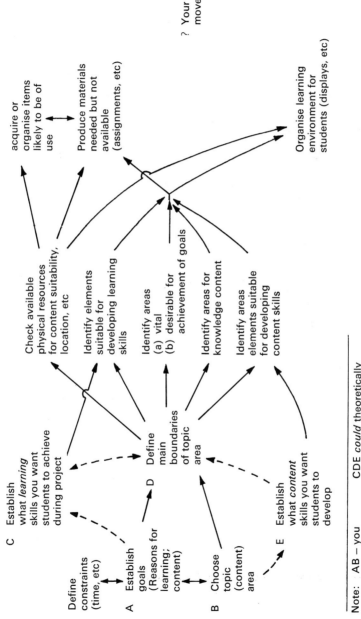

? Your move

acquire or organise items likely to be of use

Produce materials needed but not available (assignments, etc)

Organise learning environment for students (displays, etc)

Check available physical resources for content suitability, location, etc

Identify elements suitable for developing learning skills

Identify areas
(a) vital
(b) desirable for achievement of goals

Identify areas for knowledge content

Identify areas elements suitable for developing content skills

C Establish what *learning* skills you want students to achieve during project

Define main boundaries of topic area

Define constraints (time, etc)

A Establish goals (Reasons for learning; content)

D

B Choose topic (content) area

E Establish what *content* skills you want students to develop

Note: AB – you can either do these first

CDE *could* theoretically be done in any order depending on your emphasis

(3) *You may want to use the diagram as a tool for analysing particular lines of enquiry and their implications.*
You can do this in two ways.

(1) You can convert the 'information twigs' on the end of each branch into a checklist of questions for the student to answer — or for you to apply either to designing or to checking assignments: an example will be found on p 73.

   The advantages of this are that it is a familiar approach for the user and that there are a series of direct questions to answer. The disadvantages are that it *may* inhibit him in further exploration and that it tends to take up a good deal of space.

(2) You can simply 'convert' the organised coral diagram into what amounts to a radial diagram,
   by (a) sorting the branches into a logical order
      (b) arranging for the 'user' to work round the diagram considering any factors and their connections as he does so. An example will be found on p 176.

The advantages are that it is very compact — you can put all the information 'researched' by four or five pages of checklists on one page, it also allows the user to explore a considerable number of variables while acting as an aide-mémoire to ensure that he does not leave anything important out. Its disadvantage is that it is an unfamiliar format and requires some skill or practice in classifying to use well.

In either case, once again, you have a useful basis for constructing assignments where you want the student to investigate a number of similar items, for example, or where you want to give selective guidance while seeing what implications that may have!

On the next page are:

(1) a partly drawn radial diagram based on the geographical example for a local land-use project mentioned in Chapter 6

(2) a skeleton set of questions which could be derived from it.

NB for clarity only certain factors are shown: one could clearly develop particular 'arms' according to the learning requirements.

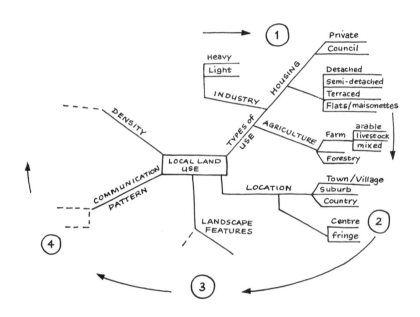

This could be expressed as a series of checklists under headings. For example,

What is the land used for:
is it industrial? If so, light or heavy industry?
                    What exact type of industry?
is it for housing? If so, is it council housing?
                    private housing?
                    is it detached house(s)?
                    semi-detached?
                    terraced?
                    flat, maisonettes?